HOW TO LIVE
WITH YOUR CHILDREN
AND LIKE THEM

Clyde F. Boyle, Michael C. Boyle, David E. Boyle

Library of Congress Catalog Card Number: 76-28860

ISBN 0-88494-308-9

First Printing, 1976

Second Edition, 2002
by The Learning Crew, Sandy, Utah

Lithographed in the United States of America
PUBLISHERS PRESS
Sail Lake City, Utah

Preface

From the glittering courts of Solomon emerged phenomenal advice in volumes of verse. Perhaps one of the most profound proverbs concerned that all-important area of child-rearing, "Train up a child in the the way he should go: and when he is old, he will not depart from it."

As over-simplified as that counsel might sound, it works! And it is my contention that the exciting role of parenthood can also be simple if approached correctly. Parenthood need not be as complex as many psychologists and scholars represent it to be.

The principles of effective parenting do not come as a natural endowment, however. They must be learned and developed just like any other skill or talent. Thus this book is written with a twofold purpose: first, to teach the *basics* of effective child-rearing; and second, to give parents the *confidence* they need to change child-rearing from a burden to a delight.

This book is not intended to be an academic textbook. Chapters are purposely brief; statistics are dispensed with; and psychological jargon is avoided. It is not written to the scholar but to parents, who can sit with it during moments of leisure and gain encouragement and direction without wading through non-essentials.

It is my hope that this book will provide simple, easy-to-digest guidelines to parents, offering them workable solutions in problems of child-rearing. If, like Solomon's advice, the concepts seem over-simplified, my advice is to try them. Parents will be delighted and amazed to find that, in this as in other aspects of living, it is often the simple truths which are the most meaningful.

Acknowledgements

A book such as this one is seldom possible without friends, family and colleagues who believe in the author's cause and lend it full support. For their suggestions, help and encouragement I extend acknowledgment and appreciation to the following:

My sons, Michael, David, and Scott, who assisted me in writing this book and who are now pursuing this same field of study through private practice and advanced degrees.

Emerson West, who played a vital part in encouraging me to write this book and then offering invaluable assistance.

Nancy Wudel and Barbara B. Baker for editorial work.

And, of course, my choice friend, companion and wife, Lettie, for her constant support and patience and for that major motivation to write the book—her conviction that parents are in great need of the supportive help it embodies.

How to Live with Your Children and Like Them

Contents

How to Live with Your Children and Like Them

Chapter 1
Understanding the Behavior of Children

A philosopher once penned the words, "Produce great pumpkins—the pies follow!"

And so it is, in a sense, with parenthood. Parents are in the process of producing "great pumpkins." Yet some parents expect the immediate enjoyment of the pie. They fail to study the art and techniques of rearing children; they try to train their children without purposeful plans of action, but then expect the children to show immediate results of good behavior and outstanding capabilities.

Training children is a huge investment of time and effort. It usually takes a long time to see the results. To be successful in any profession we must first do a certain amount of homework to get a basic knowledge of the subject. Likewise we must be trained in parenthood before we can successfully and enjoyably train children.

1

Put two struggling parents together and the dialogue is usually the same. "Timmy knows he isn't allowed to play in the street. I know he does it to test me!" Or, "Why does Robyn keep acting like that? She knows she is going to get a spanking."

The perennial questions of parenthood are: Why do children misbehave? Is it to get attention? Is it to chop down parents? Is it a lack of love? Just what is the reason?

One desperate mother even exclaimed: "I used to worry about getting wrinkles. Now that's the least of my worries. I just worry about getting through motherhood sane!"

As parents truly come to understand children's behavior and what goes on behind the scenes of a child's stageplay, they realize that parenthood need not be a struggle with sanity but can be a delightful and peaceful experience. That's not to say that the rewards, the fulfillment, and the "pie" come without hard work and organization, but they can come in a happy and enjoyable way. Parenthood can mean much more than merely bouncing from one pressure point to another.

As a parent peeks backstage, he finds that the child's testing, fudging or pressing is not for any of the standby reasons (getting attention, cutting parents, lack of love). Rather they are for what some psychologists label "clarification."

Often parents are unstable and inconsistent in their demands and expectations. Thus children misbehave as a subconscious reaction to inconsistency and confusion. Although they are not consciously aware of it, they are calling for clarification, for a clear setting down of standards and limitations.

Sometimes children misbehave because they are hungry, tired, uncomfortable or selfish. But more often than not they are really crying for someone to take control, to stand by standards, to give some direction.

As we analyze society, we find little or no stability in institutions outside the home. Since we have few stable guides to follow in modern society, it is as important as it is natural that standards for living, stability, should come from the family unit. Here it is that children seek it.

Behavior and standards are learned and taught from the environment around us. They are not inherited through chromosomes and genes. Good behavior is taught and learned just as are the skills of reading and writing.

A mother would never hand a book to her child and say: "You must learn to read. You have seen me read. Your brother Tom knows how to read and you must learn, too."

Intentionally or not, this is the approach many parents use in teaching their children proper behavior. Some parents even go so far as to add, in effect, "I'm right here beside you, but please don't ask me for help."

If a child is to learn good behavior, he must be *taught* the basics of good behavior just as he must be taught the basics of reading. A parent could give her first-grade child a reader and let him carry it around, let him eat and sleep with it, and then pour into the child all the love the parent could muster; but the child still would not learn to read until someone actually taught him the basic mechanics of reading. Only then would he be able to understand what reading is all about.

So it is with growing up—with learning to get along with brothers and sisters, learning responsibilities, or learning to control emotions and actions. If a child is to learn these behavioral skills, someone must be willing to teach him on a consistent basis. Children are not wise enough or stable enough to find proper directions of behavior without someone pointing the way.

So we get back to the perennial question: Why do children misbehave? The answer is: Because, right or wrong, they function the way they have learned.

To more successfully digest the ideas of this chapter, we might mentally change the name of the chapter to "Understanding the Behavior of Parents."

To simplify matters, let's focus on three general types of parents, because that is where the most common behavioral problems with children occur. Strangely enough, most parents do fit somewhere in these three categories.

First, the *resentful* parent.

For too long in our society we have been saying to parents that if you just love your children and family, be

4

kind, considerate, and long-suffering, you will not have problems. This concept is not true, because we are all subject to the stress and strain around us, and learning itself creates problems. If a child is out of control and is "bugging" his parents continually, the parents will usually develop *feelings of resentment.*

In our society, we are taught that it is not normal for parents to resent their children, so when it happens guilt feelings erupt within the adult. To salve those feelings and soothe their consciences, Mom and Dad find themselves making up to the child by being over-permissive. This makes them ineffective in teaching and adds to the child's confusion.

Second, the *"feeling sorry"* parent.

Some parents feel sorry for their children for various reasons. A parent might feel sorry for a child because of his poor health, or because the child is ugly, physically handicapped, or has undesirable personality traits. A mother may feel sorry for giving birth to a child who was not wanted or expected. She might feel sorry because her husband does not measure up to her expectations of a father.

One might think at face value that it would be the saintly thing for parents to feel sorry for their children. But it is almost impossible for a parent to teach when he feels sorry for a child. Why? Because these feelings tend to make parents over-indulging. They allow, condone, put up with. Again, they are being basically too permissive.

These parents do not hold the child accountable for his actions or responsibilities. They pick up the slack and do for him. Therefore their ability to teach him is almost nil.

Another problem in this situation is that the child himself knows he is treated differently and can easily develop self-image problems. He might allow his special treatment but resent it and then express his resentment by improper behavior.

Third, the *inconsistent* parent.

How many have heard the mother yell through the house to her children, "I told you, we don't yell in the house." Alternatively, how about the mother who pulled down her child's pants, and as she whacked her, scolded, "Bad girl for hitting!" When the punishment was over, the child turned on the mother and, through her tears, sobbed, "Bad Mommy for hitting!"

There is a security in knowing where you stand in a relationship with someone else. Without realizing it an inconsistent parent invites the child to press or push on each situation that arises in their relationship. This pattern starts early in childhood and is learned through the years.

If the messages a child gets are always changing, the child learns that he cannot depend on his parents. The only alternative left is to push to find out what they really mean. "How far can I go with you, Mother?

Where are the limits? You have said no, I can't go to the movies, but I don't believe you really mean no. If I mount a little pressure, I can change no to yes."

Parents might think that a child delights in this kind of behavior, but this is not so. He is not happy functioning in this manner. Why is he not happy? Because children, like adults, create conflict in the world they live in when they allow themselves to lose control of their emotions, actions, or feelings.

No one can find happiness in that atmosphere, whether it is inner or outer conflict. The moment a person finds himself in conflict, he becomes full of anxieties. Along with anxieties comes fear. He fears that he may have pushed too far and the whole roof will tumble in. Nevertheless he will endeavor to discover how far is too far. In addition, guilt feelings arise in the person who has misbehaved or gone out of control. The package of emotional disturbance, anxiety, and anger creates a psychological trauma in the child which is very damaging to him.

The serious concern is that the child may take these emotional traumas with him into adulthood, into the standard relationships in life—his relationship with his marriage partner, his next-door neighbor, his employer, and so on.

Children find security around consistent guidelines and limits they can count on, depend upon, and plan on. The opposite situation, when children have no set limits, can be compared to an automobile driver going along the highway on a dark, stormy night without a lane divider to indicate where the automobile's position should be in relation to the other cars. Panic and confusion flood the driver's mind.

The driver experiences a great sense of relief when out of the darkness looms a white line or a divider lane to follow. This leads him to safety. The world seems brighter and he can relax and settle down to go on with the business of the evening.

Another illustration is traveling the Bay Bridge between Oakland and San Francisco. The first time you cross over that body of water is a rather frightening experience.

When the journey starts there is no turning back, as the traffic literally pushes you along.

Thoughts pass through your mind of what would happen if you ran out of gas or had a flat tire, or if someone bumped into you high above the water and pushed you over the side. As you journey along, however, you see the steel railings or limits on the side structure. This immediately gives you a feeling of security.

You know that if your problems become too great and you are not able to cope with them on your own, these guidelines or limits will be there to support and protect you. Take away these steel railings and leave nothing but the flat surface and the bridge would be too frightening to cross.

Children likewise need guidelines or limits to strengthen and protect them until they have learned to cope properly by themselves.

A beautiful twenty-four-year-old young woman came into my office for therapy. She was very troubled and depressed. She had become pregnant while unmarried three times and was in this condition again. She told me that no one really cared about her as a person. Yet phone calls from concerned relatives in three different cities had come into the office. When I asked her to explain this, she indicated that during a crisis the loved ones rallied to her support, but that in the interim they just let her go.

Then she recounted an experience from her junior high school days. She was going around with a group of friends that were a very bad influence on her. She wanted to break the relationship with them, but didn't have the personal strength to do so.

She decided on a plan. She would take her friends home to let her mother and father see their kind of behavior, and she knew the parents would prohibit her from seeing them again. Into the home these youngsters came with their cigarettes and beer. They were loud and boisterous. They sat down and began talking. The father and mother walked to the closet, put on their coats, and left for a drive, leaving their daughter to cope with the visitors on her own.

When she finished this story she turned to me and said, "If they really loved me, they would have stopped me when I was not able to handle the situation on my own."

A parent needs to understand how damaging permissiveness can be. If a child can manipulate and maneuver the parent, the child loses admiration, respect and love for him. When this happens, the child usually says that no one really cares or is concerned.

On the other hand, the parent who is significant in his child's life develops a relationship of admiration, respect, and love. *By his actions* a wise parent gives the child the feeling that someone is interested in him and loves him.

Charles Dickens once said of children, "I love these little people; and it is not a slight thing, when they who are so fresh from God love us."

As parents seek for effective ways to return love to a child, they do well to realize that love is more action than words. For that action to have long-lasting effects for good, parents must honestly seek to understand their child's behavior and then commit themselves to implement firm and consistent plans of action.

Chapter 2

How to Discipline Children

In the world of parent and child, no word is more misunderstood or more misused than the word *discipline.*

Many parents equate discipline with punishment, and, sometimes, punishment with pain. The word *discipline* really means receiving instruction from another, correcting, molding, or strengthening.

In other words, it means to *teach.* There is little or no teaching taking place by a parent who feels the need to punish or inflict pain when a child misbehaves. When children misbehave frequently, they are unable to control their emotions, actions, or feelings.

We have all seen the father who yells repeatedly at his child, "Stop crying!" as the child only cries harder and harder.

Actually, a child is crying for someone to help him take control and set limits for him rather than indulge in the interplay or put up with it. To stop the action is not

11

punishment but love, because uncontrolled emotions are damaging to the child and those around him. A permissive parent allows the child to get out of control and stay there until the situation reaches an emotional crisis wherein both child and parent end up in tears.

A parent needs to be able to say to himself: "I love you too much to let you damage yourself by getting out of charge. Whatever it costs, I am willing to pay to stop it." To put up with, ignore, or compete only feeds the fire. When Johnny gets a whim, thought or desire and lets go of his negative feelings and emotions, it leads into conflict. The loving parent will help him take control, thus offering support and protection.

An old Chinese proverb says, "Better for a child to cry than his parents." Parents must remember that misbehavior is not a stage. It is not something the child will outgrow. There is no better or easier time than now to stop misbehavior, because if the child does not learn to control his emotions when he is young his problems and misbehavior will only get worse as he gets older.

One common stumbling block that stands in the way of parents effectively disciplining and teaching their children is a negative emotional involvement which causes guilt within a parent. Seeing a child angry or resentful will often send the mother into a guilty despair. Feelings such as these fill her mind:

(1) It's really my fault. I should spend more time with Susie.

(2) I should be more chummy.

(3) I should love Susie more to correct the situation.

(4) I should listen to her more.

If these thoughts enter the mother's mind when the misbehavior starts, the mother is on the road to causing more misbehavior. If she could see the problem realistically and not emotionally, she would find that Susie's problem is not a lack of love or understanding, or the need for a listening ear or a chummy companion. It is simply that she is misbehaving.

If mother would stop the misbehavior she then could teach Susie a better way to act, and both mother and child would be happier with their relationship.

This brings us to the million-dollar question: "How do I stop the misbehavior?"

Again, before that question is answered, I must reiterate that parents can be told ways of stopping misbehavior, but these will not be effective until the parents can free themselves from the emotional involvement mentioned above. If they do feel sorry or guilty, they can use many methods and gimmicks but none will really work. Susie will sense Mother's unsureness from her tone of voice and facial expressions, and she will continue to push as her behavior gets worse and worse. If a parent will detach himself from feeling guilty or sorry he will become sure and confident and can help his child take control.

One of the most effective methods of helping Susie take control when she is misbehaving is to give her a "time-out place" where she is to go and think about her problem until she has it under control. That means she is *isolated from the rest of the family* or "benched" from the ball game until the anger, lackadaisical attitude, foolishness, or disobedience is gone and she is able to act in a more worthwhile manner.

When benching a child, it is important not to place a time limit. If you do, Susie will think she is there only to serve time rather than to put herself together emotionally. The purpose of "benching" is to teach the child to control his feelings and actions.

So Susie is to stay on the bench until she can prove to Mother that she is in control again.

The benching location is important. Don't send Susie to her room, as parents often do, where there may be many things to distract her from thinking through the problem—playing with toys, listening to the radio, or even going to sleep. There she can escape from the problem rather than solve it. So the time-out place should be fairly free of distractions.

Often prison inmates coming from county jails say: "Okay, I broke a law and the only difficulty was that I got caught. Now, I'm here to be punished, so I'll take my punishment and serve this five-year sentence placed upon me. When I've completed my punishment, and the slate has been wiped clean, I'll go out and do it again." They see the incarceration period as a punishment rather than as an opportunity to change their basic behavior and personality patterns.

If a child can gain control in five minutes, he should not be benched for forty-five minutes. If the child stays too long on the bench the process will turn from learning control to punishment. If the child is let off the bench before he has resolved the problem, the process would be a waste, with child winning and parent losing.

While the child is in the time-out box or benched it is important that he not be involved with anyone or anything. The family goes on about their business and he is not a part of the group. If he is allowed to talk with them or given something to play with or do, it will hinder him from working through the problem. When the child wants to come off the bench the adult should first draw some commitments from the child. For example, the conversation might go like this:

"Mother, I want to get off the bench. I'm tired of sitting here."

"Good, Susie, you want to get off and I would like to have you off, but first I want to know how you are going to act."

If Susie tells her mother how she will act it will mean much more than having the mother tell the child, because Susie will be committing herself to the solution. When Mother does the telling, the child is not committed. Oftentimes Susie is not buying what Mother is selling and will make no effort to comply.

For some children who are quite disturbed, their commitment to take control will only last for a few minutes and they will then begin building up again for another explosion. The parent should be aware of this build-up early and say, in effect: "Look, I sense that you are starting to get upset or out of control, and this is too damaging to you and me. So will you put yourself together and take control or will I have to take control for you? I would rather you do this on your own, but if you do not, I'll have no choice and so it will be back to the bench again."

As parents become consistent with this, the mis-management of the child will become less frequent until it will finally phase out entirely. On the other hand, if they are inconsistent and only follow through now and again, the pattern will not jell and Susie will not improve.

Teaching by having a time-out place in which the child is to gain control is usually more effective emotionally for everyone concerned than paddling or spanking.

Spanking usually results from parents losing control. They get so angry before trying to set limits that they tend to spank too hard. After the cooling-off process they feel very guilty for causing physical pain and then try to make up to the child by over-indulging again. This process is not only a waste but it confuses the child.

Spanking can be effective as a tool instead of a weapon, if it is used for teaching when the child refuses to hear or listen and continues on and on "out of control."

16

It should *never* be used to punish or get even, or to make the child *pay* by creating pain. It should not be used as a way for parents to let out their frustrations.

Discipline, not punishment, should be part of the schooling process. All parents' efforts should be directed toward teaching the child and changing his personality traits for the better. And this can only be achieved when both parent and child are in control of their emotions, actions, and feelings.

Now let's consider these discipline methods in relation to two special groups: children with behavior disorders and teenage children.

In group therapy sessions, these two questions often arise:

"But what about my child with behavior disorders? He's a special case."

"Your methods are fine for young children, but how do I bench my teenager?"

On the surface, both categories may seem to require a different approach. Basically, however, discipline principles and patterns are the same as those already discussed.

First, children with behavior disorders.

A highly nervous child with a short attention span who is constantly "on the go" may be labeled as "hyperactive" and similar disorders, causing great dismay to adults and children alike. It isn't unusual to find two or three of these children in each school class of twenty-five. They are very disruptive to the teacher or parent. They destroy lesson activities. They create a noisy atmosphere that tends to ignite other children. And, most of all, they are incapable of learning the subject matter because they are too emotionally disturbed to comprehend the material being presented. These children usually have average or better-than-average intelligence, but they are not able to use their native intelligence to recall or absorb the subject matter being taught.

In desperation the schools look to the medical profession for help, if for no other reason than to contain the child and get relief from an exasperating situation. The medical profession has tried to respond to the schools' frantic plea for help by providing medicine to the hyperactive child.

Medication for a child is sometimes necessary for a while to help the child exist and function in the school atmosphere. But it does nothing to remedy the basic cause of hyperactivity. Under medication the child becomes lethargic, but as the medication wears off, the nervousness appears again without any improvement in the behavior.

The kind parent or teacher will protect the hyperactive child from himself by not allowing the misbehavior to continue. And here is where "benching" can be an effective solution. For a hyperactive child, providing a "time-out room" might be easier than the bench for the parent or teacher. But the most important requirement is for the adult to help the child take control when he is getting out of control and can't handle the situation on his own. The adult must provide a place for the child to remain until his emotions are under control and he is able to function once again. If the adult is consistent with this procedure and looks upon it as helpful and not punitive, kind and not mean, the child will eventually learn to control himself on his own. He will settle down, relax, and feel better as a person.

Parents whose children have symptoms of this nature should in most cases be given professional help rather than let the child continue to fail in normal situations of life. Failure experiences typical of the hyperactive child can be very damaging emotionally and mentally. But there is a word of caution: In seeking help, parents should find professionals trained in the mental health of children. Under such supervision, success in dealing with hyperactivity can be realized much more rapidly and effectively.

Second, disciplining the *teenager*.

There are too many teenagers who operate out of control at the expense of their families. They intimidate their families and cause their parents to feel helpless to discipline them. Some parents fear their teenagers for their physical stature or their abusive language.

Teenagers who continually misbehave set poor examples for younger children, frustrate their parents, and generally make difficult demands on the family.

I saw a family in therapy who was frightened of their seventeen-year-old son, Marvin. If Marvin was deprived of the family car, he would react by kicking the walls or breaking the windows. This would cause the father to panic and compromise by giving up the automobile.

This is an extreme case, but nevertheless such cases and similar ones do exist in some families. And using the benching method is not very realistic here!

What is to be done in such a case? Obviously the parents need supportive help to set limits they are not able to provide on their own. As unappealing as it may sound, effective and valuable help frequently can come from an outside agency such as the police department or juvenile hall. In some localities a private school or institution is available to give twenty-four-hour supervision until the child is willing to take control of himself. Again this is a supportive act to protect the child from himself when he is in danger of damaging himself and those around him.

The kind person is the one who will stop the interplay rather than condone it or put up with it and thus allow the problem to increase. Families that truly desire to stop misbehavior can confidently close the door to their teenager and not allow him to be part of the family unit until he can convince the parents that he is willing to function as a worthwhile family member. Then and only then will the behavior begin to change for the better. If a youngster is incarcerated at an institution he should remain there until he can convince the parents that he is willing to take control of his emotions and actions. To let him return home without some definite commitments of change would be a total waste of the experience.

Where a teenager is less disturbed than Marvin but still is abusive of a family privilege, such as driving the family car, Father should simply take charge. In the instance of the automobile, he should pick up the keys and take control of them. It would not be long until the teenager would be asking for the use of the car.

Father then could look at the problem with his son by saying: "You want to use the car, and I would like you to use it. I'm tired of chauffeuring you about town, and you will not learn responsibility unless you have the opportunity to try. However, my concern is how well you will handle this privilege. If I give you the keys, does this mean you will snatch the car without proper consent and abuse the opportunity of driving it? Or will you manage your desires to use it only with prior approval from us?"

The father looks at the problem with his son and draws from him commitments of change. If the child, rather than the parent, verbalizes the change, he is basically more a part of the agreement and can be held accountable for the commitments he makes.

If the father does not get the commitments he wants and needs, he tells his son that he (the son) is not convincing and will have to forego the privilege of the car until he can persuade the parents that he will perform according to family standards. If the parent feels, however, that the child is honestly sincere in wanting to change his behavior pattern, he should be given the opportunity to try.

After getting a commitment, still another step is essential if the process is to be meaningful. When the son returns home with the car there must be an accounting as to how well he has performed according to his agreements. If he phases back into the home without such an accounting, the act of getting a commitment will be wasted.

This process of controlling the situation by withdrawing privileges, in a supportive and not punitive way, is very effective in teaching a teenager the importance of accountability and of earning, not expecting, pleasures and rewards.

Again, correct principles of proper behavior and discipline lie in both the parent and the child learning to control emotions, actions, and feelings.

Chapter 3

Guide to Success
in Schools

"Mrs. Lewis," an anxious voice began on the other end of the phone, "this is the high school counselor. I'm afraid we have a serious problem with your son, Robert..."

So unfolds a story, typical of situations throughout the country, of a young teenager whose file is finally stamped "Dropout."

Every year, scores of high school students leave school permanently, usually around the sophomore or junior year, because they cannot successfully meet the challenge of formal education; they simply cannot cope. Some manage to become successful in establishing worthwhile livelihoods, while others never do measure up and drift from one failure experience to the next.

Case histories usually repeat themselves, as in the reaction of Robert's mother, "But his father and I can't understand how this could happen. What went wrong?"

The casual observer—teacher, counselor, or even parent—is usually not aware of what is happening until the child stops coming to school. The roots of failure originate early in childhood, however. Let's whirl back in time and look at Robert's childhood, ten years before the problem surfaced.

Robert's mother was like any other well-meaning, conscientious parent concerned that her child be properly dressed, fed, and cared for. Since Robert was her last child, she felt he was her "baby." She desired to be such a good mother that she began taking over Robert completely as he turned three, four, and five. She dressed him, fed him, picked up his toys, and waited on him hand and foot.

Now let's stop the picture here, because this is where the damage began for Robert and where problems take root for many children.

Remember Disney's classical "Cinderella"? Recall the scene of Cinderella helping her stepsisters prepare for the ball. The mean stepsisters' demands were incessant: "Wash this slip!" "Press this dress!" "Curl my hair!" "Find my fan!"

Many mothers, like Robert's, nobly assume the role of Cinderella to their children; meeting every demand while fallaciously thinking that they are being diligent mothers. The truth is that the very act of catering to the child's every need teaches false and dangerous principles. Doing things for a small child which he can do for himself with practice and desire, teaches the child that someone else will do tasks and chores for him if he chooses not to do for himself.

When we expect very little or nothing from a child, he gives us very little or nothing in return. In this way both parent and child lose in the end. The child is not taught responsibility, how to follow directions, or how to complete tasks and assignments. And the mother finds herself saying: "I'll be glad when my children are grown. I never stop!"

As a result of Mother's assuming an improper role, she may begin nagging the child. The child sees himself failing in each situation because he has not been taught how to invest himself. If Mother assumes that her rightful role is to pick up after a child, she fails to teach the child that he is accountable for his own actions.

David O. McKay, a prominent religious leader, once explained: "The child should learn that there are limits to his actions; that there are certain bounds beyond which he cannot pass with impunity... 'Train up a child in the way he should go; and when he is old, he will not depart from it...' In this old adage the word *train* has great significance."

The end result of improper training and misdirected mothering is a failure experience for the child. If he is not taught responsibility at home and how to follow directions, he will fail in similar situations at church and school. One cannot fail time and time again and still have a good self-image or sense of well-being. Failure breeds feelings of frustration, hopelessness or helplessness. As this goes on through the years, the child who has not learned discipline, responsibility, and accountability in his very early years will withdraw or phase out rather than take the chance of trying and failing. Children may handle failure by resorting to clowning and horseplaying, or by becoming resentful and refusing to function. These insecurities will inevitably surface into more serious problems further down the road.

"Mommy, when can I go to school?" is the eager cry of the four-year-old. Almost all children are delighted to attend kindergarten and first grade because of the prestige and status that comes with school. It is usually presented to them as fun and games. Yet as they attend school they often become disillusioned because they find that school is hard work if they are to learn and compete successfully. They are expected to complete assignments, do things for themselves and progress with the class.

The child who has not adequately learned these skills at home will daydream, ignore, and put off. He has no other choice because he has not learned how to cope with the situation. He may be part of the class physically, but his mind is wandering elsewhere, fantasizing of faraway places and of more pleasant things, not aware of what the teacher is presenting. The process of "dropping out" has begun!

Phasing out or withdrawing can also be classified with daydreaming. Daydreaming can be restful if one doesn't go there too often and stay too long. It can be an escape mechanism when the load is too heavy to carry, whereby one can replenish his well-being by living vicariously through make-believe experiences. But when an adult or child constantly resorts to daydreaming he can lose his self-identity in the real world.

I once asked my clients where they daydream the most. Seventy percent of the group said they daydream more in church than in other places. Exploring the reasons, they concluded that they were not held accountable verbally for what was being said from the pulpit. They did not have to recall or remember important ideas presented, so the mind could wander from reality without any immediate consequence.

Then I asked the question: Where do you daydream the least? The answers were all the same. It was when they were given direct instructions from an employer, principal, or supervisor, because they knew they would be held accountable for the assignments with direct results expected. Under this pressure, their minds came back to reality and began to function.

It is the same with children. Again, where little or nothing is expected, little or nothing is accomplished. Almost every teachers' conference or inservice meeting emphasizes the importance of making learning fun and interesting so that the student will want to learn. This is fine, but it is sometimes too one-sided. The reality is that learning basically requires work. A child must put forth as much effort as the teacher if he is to develop basic skills—fun or not.

Adults are required to perform at certain work levels in life whether they are motivated or not, or whether it is fun or not. And a child must gradually and thoroughly learn this principle too, if he is to function successfully as an adult.

I was once called to consult with a seventh-grade reading teacher of educationally handicapped children. The teacher was in tears trying desperately to develop "fun" games to encourage a certain boy to read. All the while he was ridiculing her efforts. I said to the teacher, "You are staying up until midnight working on lesson plans to bring this skill into Raymond's life, but how much effort is Raymond putting into the process?"

The teacher's mouth dropped as she admitted that his efforts were nil.

"Well, then, under these conditions you can be assured that Raymond will not learn to read even though he has above-average intelligence."

The teacher learned a great truth. If a child is not held accountable for what happens in school, he simply will not invest; if he will not invest himself, he will not learn; and if he does not learn, he will not have a success experience in school.

Let's consider a typical public school experience:

For homework, Mrs. Thompson assigns ten arithmetic problems which are to be corrected by the students the next day in class. She has thirty-four students and feels it impossible to correct personally each paper in each subject matter she teaches.

Bethany, who is in the class, completes only two of the assigned problems. She feels no external pressure to push to complete the assignment because there is no accounting with parent or teacher to see if the assignment was finished. No one is checking to see how well the assignment was done or if Bethany understood the process involved. Since Bethany does not have to account to anyone, she finds it easy to drift out to sea mentally.

With arithmetic, like most subject matter, if you miss out in one step of problem solving, the entire process can become a muddle. So Bethany misses a step, lacks the motivation to seek help, and begins phasing out.

This case is a common one, and the process of "phasing out" is becoming a serious problem in public education.

So now comes the question: What can be done?

The answer is one simple concept: *Teamwork*. Generally, in schools there is no follow-through or working relationship between teacher and parent, other than an annual parent-teacher day. Schools are expected to do it alone, to produce intelligent, controlled children regardless of parental support. The result? More failure; jails and mental hospitals called into service, and welfare rolls backlogged. No public school, Sunday School, church or youth activity program can do it alone. There must always be informed parents and concerned teachers who work together to help a child cope with the real world and its demands before he escapes to drugs, alcohol, dropping out, and more.

David O. McKay also said that "in the ideal state, the teacher would be the parents' ally, training the mind, encouraging worthy habits and fostering noble traits of character inculcated by wise parental teaching and example." Thus the child's chances of succeeding in school are much greater with parent and teacher supporting each other.

Generally, students do not come home and inform parents that they did poorly in their studies or failed tests. If parents were to ask, they would be vulnerable to accept whatever information the child shares, accurate or not. Parents want to hear good reports, so the child usually gives success stories, only to have the parents disillusioned ten weeks later when report cards tell a different story.

But if schools had a consistent method of reporting to the parents, each day if necessary, the progress and development of the student would be enhanced. If ten arithmetic problems were assigned and only one or two were completed, the parents would need to know of this situation that very day in order to bring the task to a conclusion. If parents would follow through with a check each day to make sure that all homework was completed, all the escape hatches would be buttoned down and the Bethanys and Roberts would have no place to hide. Consequently, they would begin to achieve; and as they began to achieve, failure would turn into success.

When one suggests this kind of checkup and follow-through, the teacher seems overwhelmed at the thought of doing this for each student in class. In elementary school, it would mean checking up on as many as twenty-five or thirty students in one day. In junior high or high school, it could mean as many as thirty students per class, with five or six different classes a day. This of course would be impossible. But I am not suggesting a check on every student. This process would apply only to those who are floundering and having difficulty. Those who are making it on their own do not need this supportive help.

To expect a problem student to take control of the problem on his own and turn himself around under his own power is not realistic. Usually, he is not wise enough, mature enough, or stable enough to pull himself out of his dilemma without limits and guidelines.

When parents and teachers start a process of reporting, the student's initial reaction may be rebellion. He may feel hopeless, helpless, not trusted; and he may even become defiant. The kind parent and teacher will persist, however, consistently working with the child to train him to settle down and perform. The teacher or parent should always keep in mind that the end results of these controls will be the child's achievement and happiness.

A word of caution is necessary. As the pattern improves, adults may tend to let up, slack off, and become inconsistent. When this happens, the student senses the change in attitude and drifts back to his former ways. The adult's method of helping should be consistent for many months or a year; and then he should let up gradually, with the student being fully aware of the gradual relaxation of rules. The student should be given the opportunity to explore within him whether he is now mature enough to handle the responsibility on his own. If he is honest and sincere in wanting to try, he should be given the opportunity. But if he starts to fail or to phase out again, the limits and reporting system should be reestablished until he finally learns self-discipline.

What might seem painful at first to parent, child, and teacher will nevertheless produce painless years further down the road. The Roberts, Raymonds, and Bethanys may fight and struggle against control, discipline, and accountability. But as they mature into high school, college, and finally adult living, they will find their lives' experiences stamped "high achiever," instead of "dropout"!

Aristotle touched upon the vast importance of these principles when he said, "All who have meditated on the act of governing mankind have been convinced that the fate of empires depends upon the education of youth!"

Chapter 4
The Timid, Shy Child

The English poet Wordsworth once said that "a timid person is one with more soul in his face than words on his tongue."

Yet how often misunderstood is the timid, shy child!

In our society we have many children who are shy; not because that is their normal personality, but because they are troubled and frightened. This is the group we are discussing in this chapter. There are many children who do not show their problems outwardly but keep them inside, fearful to let their emotions or feelings be seen or felt. These children have feelings like all human beings—fear, hate, joy, happiness, anger, love—but they will not risk exposing them and may even be unable to express them.

Such people often make those around them uncomfortable because though physically present, they are unable to send signals of emotional response. Just as the timid, fearful child withdraws from the world around him, the pattern most adults use in coping with the quiet child is to withdraw also. Adults usually don't want to make any waves around them for fear that they might shatter and break.

These children can sense the anxieties or fears of the adult, so they absorb these feelings and become more anxious themselves. This unhealthy rapport leaves the child feeling strange and different.

"Alice is just like her father," one mother complained. "They never say a word. I try and try to get them to talk and communicate."

Little does this mother realize that she is doing more damage than good in her efforts, for she is falling into the "wrong way" of coping with the problem. In desperation, some adults like this mother try to make the shy, timid person into what *they* think he should be. They set the personality expectations and then call out "failure" when the child doesn't measure up.

Usually, where there is a timid or shy child there is also a parent or close relative with the same personality traits. This does not mean that these traits are inherited, but that they are learned. A frightened child often has a frightened parent, a nervous child often has a nervous parent; and without realizing it, they send these feelings and vibrations back and forth to each other. Of course, this only feeds the fire.

For example, a seventh-grade girl was having problems in relating to her peers; they were "always picking on her." Her recourse was to take flight and withdraw emotionally. Her mother was distraught, and became so worried that she could not wait for her daughter to arrive home to find out how difficult her day had been. She began meeting her daughter at the bus stop to inquire anxiously about the day and offer sympathy for the problems the girl must have encountered.

Even if the girl had experienced a relatively good day in the situation, the mother's fears and anxieties would trigger her off and she would take refuge in bed, not wanting to leave her room.

As the mother was helped to govern her emotions concerning the problem, the daughter recovered. In this case the mother was as much the problem as the shy, timid child.

When a therapist counsels a child or adult, he knows that the first rule of thumb is never to tell anyone that he cannot have a certain feeling. Emotions are very real, and every human being has feelings of fear, anger, joy, love, or pain. Learning how to manage feelings so that they are not destructive to ourselves or those around us is the secret to good mental health.

"It's a beautiful world," exclaim bumper stickers. And it is indeed a beautiful world for people who can take control of their emotions. If destructive emotions take control of an adult or child, he is not in the driver's seat and can run off the road into emotional trouble.

So in helping a shy, timid child, the teacher or parent must first put himself in control of his own emotions and then reach out to help the child take control.

A graphic example is in the case of the thirteen-year-old boy who developed an emotional build-up centered around the devil. He had read books and watched television shows which emotionally he could not handle. Fears welled up inside of him and he lost control.

One October afternoon in his school class, the teacher began reading a ghost story to the class. The boy fell from his seat to the floor, crying and shaking hysterically.

A therapy session with the parents uncovered the fact that these fears and anxieties had been growing in intensity over a three-month period. The parents' way of helping the son was to let him sleep at the foot of their bed with the house lights burning all night. Every morning when he awoke, the parents' first question was, "Did you have any visions of devils in your sleep?"

Upon one occasion, the minister had been summoned to pray the devil out of the boy. The entire family was caught up in the increasing emotional trauma.

I suggested to the parents that, in this case, the problem was an emotional one. I helped them to understand that fear is a normal part of a person's mental makeup. It is not bad or sinful, and can be constructive at times. But if it is allowed to creep into a person's psychological makeup, to overwhelm him or seize control, as with this entire family, he is subject to psychological trouble.

Gradually the parents became less tense and fearful themselves. They were able to give constructive support to their son. They were capable of helping him take control of himself. When he would go into his fearful states, they would say: "Yes, we know you are frightened and we can understand how you feel. But you have got to take control of these feelings and stop. You can still manage and function even though you have fears."

The son soon began to settle down, think more positive thoughts, and control his mind and emotions. He felt strength from his parents because they felt secure and sure in what they were saying to him.

Allowing timid or frightened children to function differently from the normal standard of behavior is damaging to them psychologically. No one finds happiness in functioning too far away from so-called normal behavior. As the family or teacher allows a withdrawn child to function differently, he will begin to feel different. He will feel that he is not like other people, and this will build in anxieties and depression.

Let's look at Keith, who was a very shy, withdrawn high school student, failing his classes year after year. He associated with no one at school, slid quietly in and out of classes with no social interaction, and never spoke to anyone.

The teachers and students were aware of his difference, so they avoided him, not knowing how to approach him or even whether they should.

In therapy session with the parents I discovered that the mother manifested many of the same mannerisms which Keith did. She was uneasy, had very little confidence, and had difficulty in expressing herself. She managed to explain that Keith had an uncle whom he resembled in looks as well as in behavior. The uncle was a loner in life, had had few success experiences, and had finally committed suicide. Keith's problems seemed so identical to those of his uncle that the parents were afraid he would take the same course.

Keith had a brother and sister who were outgoing, successful and happy. The parents had high expectations of them, and they met those expectations well. But there were no expectations or house rules placed on Keith for fear that he "couldn't handle them without breaking." The parents did not want Keith to get more depressed, so they imposed none of the restrictions on him which they did on the other children.

Keith's brother and sister were expected to get high grades, while Keith was a "D" and "F" student and on the verge of being dismissed from school. Even teachers were hesitant to require standard performance of him. All family members were expected to be on time for dinner and were chastised for missing a meal. When Keith missed dinner, nothing was said. If he was late, mother kept the dinner warm until he came home.

One night, Keith arrived home about 11:00 P.M., angry and depressed. The parents tried to comfort him, but he brushed them aside and went up to his room. Suddenly, in a fit of anger, he slammed his fist through the wall of his room.

The father, forgetting himself, dashed upstairs and, seeing what had happened, grabbed Keith by the shirt, angrily shook him, and shouted, "Don't you ever do that again in this house or I'll throw you out!"

The father left the room extremely upset over Keith and even more disturbed because it was the first time he had shown negative emotion to Keith. He felt so churned up and guilty, thinking he had destroyed his son, that he called me for an emergency therapy session.

The next day, as I saw Keith, he seemed less tense than ever before. With a smile on his face for the first time, he remarked, "You know, maybe I'm not so different because Dad got mad at me last night and threatened to throw me out if I didn't act like the rest of the family."

That was the turning point for Keith. His parents began setting limits on his behavior as a means of protecting him from himself. Keith began leaving his shell and found success replacing failure. He did not finish high school because he had failed too many classes. Instead he joined the armed forces, where he was expected to perform like anyone else. He managed well and gained confidence for the first time in his life.

This case study is an excellent example for adults who are working with a timid, shy or frightened child. It illustrates that the kind person is one who will protect the child from himself by setting limits to the child's behavior. Rather than accepting abnormal behavior, the adult must set expectations of normal behavior for the child. Then he must compliment the child wherever possible and reinforce the child's acts, rather than either ignoring him or coercing him to change.

As Wordsworth suggested, the timid child can tell us much by his very act of timidity if we have the sensitivity to listen.

Chapter 5
Religion

As discussed previously, the high school dropout presents challenges to society and public education. Likewise, the church "dropout" creates some deep anxieties and concerns with parents.

Religious people most often want their children to desire a firm conviction of their church; they want their children to find the joy and stability which they have found in living religious principles. Yet when children criticize or reject gospel teachings and resist attending church, parents' hearts are broken and psychological problems result for both parent and child.

Too many parents become frightened when their children detach themselves from religious concerns, and they tend to disintegrate, not knowing how to cope with this kind of behavior. They tend to withdraw guidelines and expectations because they are afraid that

---

Because the author's religious experiences have been primarily with The Church of Jesus Christ of Latter-day Saints *(LDS or Mormon)*, this chapter is set against that background. The one or two terms used which may be unfamiliar to the non-LDS reader are largely self-explanatory, however; and the principles discussed apply equally, of course, to people of all faiths.

to pressure their child into attending church will trigger rebellion and cause the child to reject church permanently.

How many times do we hear an adult blame his church inactivity upon a mother or father who "made" him attend church when he was young? If we accepted such stories at face value, it could throw us into a real quandary!

Let's consider the church "dropout" and dive beneath the surface to learn the real causes and solutions, as we take a look at an actual case involving two active parents and their teen-age son.

Mr. and Mrs. Anderson called me for an appointment regarding their fifteen-year-old son, Randy. They indicated that he was using drugs and had been a runaway. The parents were frantic, not knowing how to help him, and desperately turned to me for counsel.

During the first meeting, details of the story unfolded. Randy had been reared in a home where the parents were faithful in their religious duties and the children were included in their religious life. Randy had always been somewhat of a loner. He played by himself and seldom cultivated friendships.

One day Randy brought home two friends from school. They were ill-mannered and used crude language, but they had nonetheless befriended Randy.

Randy's parents were so grateful to see Randy have some companionship that they accepted the new friendships.

As one might imagine, Randy soon began to pattern his habits after those of his new friends. His attitude changed; he began striking out against family rules and customs. He refused to go to church and attend the youth functions and responsibilities there. He stayed out late with his friends, did not do homework, and began sluffing school.

Then the final blow struck. Randy's school called saying he was suspended for smoking and selling marijuana on campus. In desperation, the parents called their church leaders.

Feeling the need to help them in some way, the church leaders suggested that the solution was to love Randy through all of this and be considerate and kind so that Randy would see the good in them and eventually would want to change. He further suggested that they make no demands upon Randy's attending church, as this might sour him on religion for life.

These suggestions were followed for a time, although it broke the parents' hearts. The family would leave for church while Randy stayed in bed. When the house was vacant, he would call his friends in to smoke pot. Sometimes the boys would leave the house, piling into one car and heading into the hills. There they would roll up the windows and huddle together smoking marijuana until the air was saturated with the drug. This made a more potent effect and they could get higher on less of the drug.

At this point the parents telephoned me and desperately pleaded for help. Since Randy would not come for therapy, it was necessary to teach the parents how to help him. In Randy's case certain steps toward a solution were obvious.

Seemingly for the sake of their son, Randy's parents had withdrawn limitations and expectations by allowing him to lower his standard of friends. Then, like many parents, they reacted out of fear and withdrew the requirement that Randy attend church. They gave him total, unguided freedom to make his own choices.

The first task in helping Randy was to eliminate the so-called friends that were destroying his life. The next step was to get him back in school under close supervision by parents and teachers. The final step was to see that he attended church with the family and began functioning in his youth activities and other responsibilities there. For the first month Randy rebelled fiercely against all of this. Then, gradually as he started to invest in these activities, he began to achieve. As he began to achieve, he began to like himself and enjoy his involvement. At time of writing Randy is doing well in school, is a happy and relaxed person, and is a leader in youth activities at church. Best of all, he thinks his religion and his parents are "the greatest."

As we see in this case, too often the parents' first tendency in a stress situation is to withdraw and leave the child on his own, thinking that this is the right way to solve the problem. But the children are not wise or mature enough to make the right decisions when left to their own discretion, especially during the teenage years. And there is the beginning of a church "dropout."

How many times do we hear a disgruntled student say, "My Sunday School teacher is a bore and just not motivating"? Other times we hear young people complain that they have no friends at church, so they do not wish to attend. Some feel that the subject matter is old-fashioned; others complain that a teacher or leader was rude to them or embarrassed them. All of these excuses are used to justify becoming inactive and dropping away from church.

Let's think for a moment how parents react when the student comes home from public school with similar excuses—a dull teacher, the coach chastising him for not suiting up, no friends at school, the principal setting limits for running in the hall, and so on. Somehow parents can understand the problems at school, but they still expect the student to stay right there and work through the difficulties. Under no circumstances would a parent allow a child to make his own choice to stay home or go to school. Somehow, in school situations, the child receives strength from the parent or teacher to overcome the problems and carry on. As parents, then, we might ask ourselves why we are so comfortable about our stand in regard to school attendance and so unsure and fearful about our stand regarding church attendance.

Allowing adults or children to go on mismanaging themselves is very damaging. Many adults and children are simply not strong enough to work through their problems themselves. The kind leader and parent is one who will look at the problems squarely and provide insight, understanding, and guidelines. Ignoring, putting off, or letting things go could be rationalized as a superficial love at best. Actually it feeds the problem.

As parents begin taking confident and firm stands, motivated out of genuine love and not frustrated fear, the child will be the victor over himself and will then choose to be a part of the religious community.

Chapter 6
Your Children's Friends

The first discoveries of friendships in early childhood are exciting and thrilling moments in a child's life. No matter how close brothers and sisters may be, the making of a close friend outside the family ties is a cherished experience to children. "Mommy, Johnny wants me to come to his house!" is an elated cry for the preschool youngster. His world is expanding and he begins desiring peer acceptance and approval.

As the youngster enters school, his outside world begins to revolve almost entirely around teacher and friends. The great influence of both in the child's life should not be underestimated. As a grade-schooler approaches junior high years and then teen stages, the most important part of his world is his peers and their acceptance of him. When a seventh grader finds he is quietly being left out of the crowd's activities, his rose-colored world shatters and he may enter traumatic times. Likewise, a teenager or pre-teenager is usually very settled, happy, and confident when he feels assured that his group of friends accepts him voluntarily.

Friends play a vital part in a person's emotional and social growth from childhood to adulthood. To feel at his best, everyone has need of the companionship of others. From other people we gain reassurance, comfort, security and love. These needs are basic to every person, regardless of race, color, or background.

The roots of a child's social well-being and his ability to relate successfully to others begins not with early *outside* friendships but with *home* relationships, particularly parent-child relationships. It is especially damaging to a child to feel inhibited in expressing feelings to a parent. Every child has a basic need to run impulsively to Mommy or Daddy when he is hurt emotionally or physically. He has a need to pour out his feelings and receive understanding and comfort in return. When a child is not allowed to let out feelings of frustration, disappointment or hurt to his parents, there is a serious breakdown of a critical parent-child relationship.

When a child comes to a parent expecting comfort or help, but instead receives scolding, preaching, and emotional reaction, the child tends to withdraw from that parent as a source of strength and help. If parents refuse to listen to their child's problems, or if their marriage is under stress, it isn't unusual for him, especially in teenage years, to give up the family and go to a peer group for his comfort and well-being. He attempts to find status, security, and some kind of love from his peers that he desperately needs and should be getting from his father and mother. This peer group sometimes becomes a very hard-core unit which parents cannot penetrate. The youth cling to each other for support even though many of the things which take place within the group are very damaging, such as drugs, illicit sex, and law violations.

It is encouraging to note, however, that when the parents learn how to function in a worthwhile manner with each other and love, security and status return to the family, in most cases the teenager will leave the peer group and come back to the home.

Parents should know that it is not up to them to go out into the environment and find playmates or friends for their children. If this is done on an ongoing basis, children do not learn how to develop relationships on their own and they become social cripples. Children can find friends on their own, and they should be encouraged and expected to do so. In selecting companionship, however, the young person should be expected to find peers that meet the standards of his family. To associate and cultivate friendships that are substandard to the morals of the family can have serious consequences.

Often the child that has a poor self-image will settle for less in a relationship and will take whatever friendships he can get rather than hold out for more wholesome companionship that require more effort to cultivate. It is for this reason that many years ago young people found it so easy to relate to the "hippie" element. This group required very little or nothing of a person to join the group. They did not require cleanliness, moral standards, ambition, wisdom, good grooming, and so on. After joining the group, a person benefited very little because nothing was required or offered to build his well-being on an ongoing basis.

In every community there are many wholesome, well-adjusted, happy children, and there are also many emotionally disturbed, immature, and poorly adjusted children. All of these children can have a big influence on the lives of other children, either for good or poor behavior.

Parents would not think of standing by and letting their children play on a dangerous mountain cliff without proper footing or support. Neither would they silently stand and watch while their children disobeyed traffic rules and ran into a busy intersection crowded with fast-moving vehicles. Somehow we would be moved to stop or protect them from such dangerous situations, but too often we put up with or ignore other dangers, such as improper friends, and hope that somehow all will turn out well for the child. It seldom does.

Often, children actually want parents to set up protective measures in this area. An example is John who was trying to rid himself of a group of school chums from high school. These "chums" were known as the "cool guys" on campus, using drugs and alcohol, often disrupting class, and found in the principal's office much of the time. John felt that they were on the verge of being expelled from school entirely. He tried to avoid them but was not too successful.

One Sunday evening they arrived at his house in an old jalopy, loud and vulgar in manners and speech. John was at the curb talking with them when his father drove up in his car. Sensing that all was not well, the father suggested to John that it was too late to be out and he should say goodnight to his friends and come in the house. John objected outwardly, but father insisted and stayed near enough to walk into the garage entrance with him. As they entered the garage, out of sight and hearing of the friends, John touched his father's arm and said: "Thanks, Dad. I'm glad you came along when you did and made me come into the house. Those kids have bought a lot of marijuana, and they wanted me to go to the beach for a pot party. I didn't want to go and I didn't know how to get out of it until you came along and helped."

John could blame his nonparticipation on his father and still save face at school, since he had to be with those boys in class every day. As they associate with friends, it's often easier for children to hold their parents responsible for not being able to go somewhere or do something. This takes the pressure off themselves and they can still survive with the group. Parents should be able to allow that and feel good about accepting that kind of responsibility.

In large communities where neighbors are not acquainted with each other, it is wise for parents to become acquainted with the parents of their children's friends. To understand the background those friends come from is essential. Different families have different moral standards, habits, and customs. If your child is visiting neighbors whose standards of living are different from what you would like or expect, they are being exposed to conditions not acceptable to you. It is your duty and right to change the situation, regardless of how your children react to your insistence on knowing their friends and their families. And you need to remember that you are doing all this to help your children.

If your child objects to such "screening" this is often a good clue that things are not well in the relationship. If a good, wholesome relationship exists, there should be no objections to your checking on it. Parents should not hesitate to have their children bring home friends, and in order to get acquainted they should do it early before trouble erupts. It's easier to stop relationships in the early stages than after the friendship has gone in depth with roots that are hard to untangle.

It is unequivocally the parents' responsibility to let their children know what standards their friends must have. Then they must work consistently with the children to make sure they are choosing friends who will aid in their positive growth and development, not hinder or damage it.

Chapter 7

Quarreling, Lying, and Stealing

"One of my most precious possessions is my memory of a home in which love was supreme," said David O. McKay. "I know of no other place than home where true happiness can be found in this life." He said that he pictured heaven to be an extension of the ideal home.

He went on to explain: "If upon examination, you were to find that termites were undermining the foundation of your house, you would lose no time in having experts make a thorough examination and in having the destructive insects exterminated.

"There are destructive termites of homes, as well as houses, and some of these are backbiting, evil speaking, and faultfinding on the part either of parents or of children. Quarreling is also an evil that lowers the standards of the ideal home."

Contention with all its variations is one of the most destructive forces in home and society. Lying and stealing are only extensions of basic problems in the home environment. Some psychologists of the day would label such malfunctions as "normal." "Ignore it," they say. "It's a normal stage which children will outgrow."

The fact is that quarreling, lying, and stealing are not necessary or normal to proper growth and development and are as much a menace to society as to the home and the individuals. Almost all children have some of these feelings in their makeup. But learning to control feelings rather than letting the feelings control the person is the secret to happiness.

Quarreling, lying and stealing are very difficult acts for parents to deal with because they are not quite sure who is the culprit or exactly what the problem is that's causing the turmoil. Parents feel inadequate to deal with the situation until they find out exactly what the child did and why he did it. The child soon learns that if he does not confess to the wrongdoing, if he tells lies about the incident, he can keep the parents in a quandary, and they are not able to deal with the problem for fear of making a wrong accusation. The parents are then left hanging by a nail in the wall. The matter is never settled, the incidents not stopped, and the problem returns time and time again to irritate everyone caught up in it.

Generally in a case of contention, the parent's first questions to the children are: "'Did you do it?" or "Why did you do it?" The child's natural response is, "No, I did not," or "I don't know why I did it." In either instance Mother is left with nothing concrete to work on comfortably, and thus she turns to ridiculing, preaching, and scolding, which accomplishes nothing. The effect of her words is like pouring water on a duck's back— they don't penetrate but hit and roll off.

When parents can be freed from the fear of wrongly accusing or damaging the child, they can be effective in helping the child work through the problem. If a parent can look honestly at the problem of stealing or quarreling, he can generally tell from past experience which child is causing most of the difficulty. When an incident occurs, Mother might say *to herself*: "I don't know exactly who is at fault, and I can't find out the truth by asking Paul because he often lies to me, so I'll have to use my own judgment until the lying and quarreling stop."

To Paul, she might say: "What must I do, Paul, to change the situation? Must I get angry, must I give you a spanking, or must I bench you until you can take control of yourself? I love you too much to let you go on damaging yourself and those around you. Will you take control of yourself, or will I have to take control for you?"

This approach clearly gives Mother a direction to move in and she doesn't have to have an admission of guilt to cope with the problem.

If there is more than one child involved in the incident, she should bench the two or three she suspects and not allow herself to get caught up in the interplay as to who did what, to whom, and why.

A wise mother must remember that problems of quarreling are not who took the marbles and who gets them back, rather the problem is that Lois and Steve have lost control of their actions and emotions. This is where they need help. If a parent deals only with objects, the marble situation, for example, can be settled fairly easily, but the children will still be in angry moods and quarreling will flare up again and again. Mother will find herself putting out fires, while the children light them again just as quickly. Parents should train themselves not to look at the *incident* but at the way the children are managing themselves emotionally.

Solving problems of lying and fibbing is based on the same principles as solving quarreling. If the parent's purpose is to teach and help the child manage his feelings, it can be a meaningful experience for the child when the behavior is stopped and simply not allowed or entertained.

Generally, children tell lies when they get a lot of mileage from the lies. If they can get away with it, confuse, upset and arouse Mom and Dad, they are getting much attention and reinforcement—negative though it might be. When parents stop swallowing their children's fibs hook, line and sinker, and hold them accountable for the truth, the lying stops.

For example, in the case of Paul, mentioned earlier, the most important factor is to stop misbehavior and not accept the lying. Suppose Mother did wrongly accuse Harry and hold him accountable for the trouble because of his past record. Even if Harry is innocent this time, he sees Mother taking a concrete direction and operating out of confidence, not out of confusion. Thus he knows she means business, and the situation will still be meaningful to him. It won't be long until Harry will stop lying in other situations because he sees that he will not get any mileage out of lying and that Mother will not be fooled.

An area of behavior which causes many parents heartaches *and* headaches is that of stealing. This problem has even more serious concerns attached to it since it is punishable by state and federal laws. Parents as well as courts and agencies try to curtail the lawbreaker by punishing him for his act, but they seldom take the time to help him stop such acts in the future. They deal with the symptom (that he has stolen something) rather than the cause (that he cannot control his actions).

Children do not steal because they *need* a particular article. Usually the reason is that they get a particular thought, whim or idea to have something and just let go of their emotions and actions without considering the responsibilities or consequences. Anyone can steal if he wants to; anyone can take control of those impulses if he wants to. Children get away with things by confusing parents with such explanations as: "Oh, I couldn't help it, I wanted the toy car so much and I didn't have any money," or, "I didn't steal it; it was lying on the floor and it looked old and damaged, so I was going to play with it for a while." In accepting such a line, parents ignore and excuse the behavior of stealing, letting their children get away with it with little or no consequences.

Parents must decide that there is no reason in the world which is acceptable for stealing. When they have decided that they will not listen to excuses or reasons, the stealing stops. If they are vulnerable to reasons and excuses, and then they ignore or go along with the *child's* reasoning, the problem continues even on to adulthood.

Let's look at some typical case studies in which the problem of stealing was successfully solved. Lynda was a high school student causing considerable trouble in the locker rooms and the cafeteria. Money and articles would be taken, and eventually the finger would be pointed to her. Lynda was very callous, so it would take hours to break her down to get a confession. Only the Physical Education teacher was successful in doing this. On one occasion, Lynda stated that the reason she stole was because no one trusted her anyway.

In order to help and show their trust, school officials decided to place Lynda in charge of the cash register at the snack bar. On the third day of her employment, thirty dollars were missing from the till. A lengthy interrogation began that lasted through most of the day.

As was Lynda's custom, she finally gave up, cried, and pleaded for the school authorities not to tell her father because he was ill-tempered and would beat her.

Usually the case had been dropped on previous occasions, but this time when the school called the counselor, he suggested that they take Lynda home and let her parents "own up" to the problem. Lynda complained all the way in the car about how angry her father would be, so the school counselor had Lynda remain in the car while he first approached the father to break the news.

A well-mannered father met him at the door, and in the course of the conversation the counselor learned that Lynda had never been spanked or physically harmed by either parent. She had made up the story to get sympathy from her peers and teachers; there was simply no truth to the stories she had told. The parents felt bad that the school had not informed them of the problem much sooner so that they could have corrected the situation. Lynda's stealing stopped when there was a close liaison between the school and home to check up and follow through on each incident.

Another such case involved a frantic mother who came for therapy with her eight-year-old son, Randy. He was stealing constantly from the grocery stores and was under the threat of being placed in a detention center. I saw both Randy and his mother in therapy for about two months. The stealing began slowing up, and when there hadn't been an incident for about three weeks I asked Randy why the stealing had stopped. Randy remarked, "Mother got fed up with my stealing, and she won't allow it any more, so I had to stop."

One wonders what took that mother so long to arrive at that point. Had she taken control of the situation years before, she would not have had to endure the grief and embarrassment that plagued the family for years.

A third case involves Jimmy, whose stealing first started with small, unimportant things such as neighborhood toys which he claimed had been placed in the garbage for anyone to take. Later his parents found that he was taking his brother's and sister's lunch money from the kitchen table.

One day the principal phoned and said Jimmy had three one-dollar bills in his possession that he could not account for. The parents became worried and sought help through therapy. During the first session I asked the father how he planned on helping Jimmy. Father thought taking his allowance away would be effective. I said I didn't think that would be very meaningful, but the father wanted to try it. I saw the parents again in therapy a week later, and the stealing was still in progress. This time the parents proposed that they take television privileges away from Jimmy to stop this behavior. I suggested they were just playing games with him by using these gimmicks, but the parents were insistent on trying this method.

A week passed and Jimmy's problem was getting worse. This time his mother proposed that she have a friend, a policeman, come out and talk to him. I counseled them to deal with the problem themselves and not invite someone else to do the parenting for them. The police method was tried, however, and Jimmy received a second scolding as they drove him past Juvenile Hall to see where incorrigible children were placed for stealing. This was effective for about three days, but then more incidents occurred.

The parents came for treatment very discouraged, and I asked them how they felt about what was going on—taking time from work to come to treatment, spending money for the sessions, driving fifty miles the round trip, being embarrassed by Jimmy's behavior, and so on. Father sat up in his chair and exclaimed loudly that he was getting very tired of it all. For the first time, feelings of anger and resentment replaced his former feelings of helplessness and hopelessness. When I asked him if he could go home and show Jimmy the anger and resentful feelings he manifested in therapy, he thumped his fist on his knee and swore. "You bet I can, and I'm going home right now to do it!"

The following week both parents came for their sessions and they seemed delighted. The stealing had stopped. When I asked what had happened to cause Jimmy to stop, the father stated loudly and clearly that he had had a stomachful of that nonsense and wasn't going to tolerate stealing any more. From that point on Jimmy improved and so did his parents.

The last case is one typical of many families. Mary was only five years old and her problem of stealing was severe. Her parents would have to lock all cupboards and drawers in the house to keep her from taking things. The neighbors would not let her come into their homes to play, and the grocer finally told her mother not to bring Mary to the store again or he would have to refuse them admittance.

I saw the parents in therapy once a week for nearly two months, with no improvement in Mary's behavior. Mary was into everything, filling her pockets and making off with her loot. The parents were spanking, scolding, and taking away privileges. Finally, I asked how they felt towards the child and towards what was going on. Both parents were silent for a time, and after looking at each other, the mother responded, "We have been told that Mary is a very intelligent child, maybe a genius, and for that reason we have been fearful to stifle her inquisitiveness."

Mary could sense their unsureness in this area, even though they paddled, preached, and screamed, so the parents were not effective in helping her work through the problem. But now I was able to help the mother and father see that Mary's behavior was not being inquisitive but rather was being out-of-control. Once the parents insisted that Mary control her actions and feelings, the improvement was remarkable. As she received support from her parents in managing this problem, she was accepted at home and in the community because she was functioning in a more acceptable manner. Mary began liking herself more too as she became happier.

The lessons derived from these case studies are obvious. As parents set high standards of performance and expectations in the home environment as well as in society, and as they rigidly demand compliance with these rules, children will respond. If there is peace in the home, love will be supreme, and parents will go to great lengths to ensure that there are no permanent threats to that peaceful environment.

How to Live with Your Children and Like Them

Chapter 8

Naptime and Bedtime Hour

From man's beginning, sweet strains of gentle lullabies have soothed the young and old. For ages, a simple verse of "lullaby and goodnight..." with allusions of dreamland have sent the "little people" off into peaceful slumber.

It is with that vision of the bedtime hour that most young parents approach the close of their child's day—only to discover that sleeptime isn't always so blissful!

In reality, what is idealized as the sweet hour of the day is often far from that for several reasons: 1) normally, both parent and child are tired physically; 2) the child may resist the finality of this interruption from his play; 3) the child may be emotionally over-wrought as a result of earlier events; 4) Mom and Dad may radiate tenseness and a rushed feeling, desiring to bed down the child quickly so as to get on to other projects or commitments.

Some adults even make the mistake of looking upon children as toys or playthings rather than human beings having great potential if channeled in the proper direction. Thus some parents use the last hour of the child's day as a make-up session to do the things they failed to do with the child during the day. Dad is generally the worse culprit, since he hasn't seen his offspring "all day." He often turns the pre-bedtime hours into wrestling or roughhouse matches, with Dad geared high now that he is ready to play with his child.

What is the solution? How do parents take control in order to have the child and parent's day end on a harmonious note instead of one of discord? First, let's examine several basic "rules" of bedding down the child. It is essential that *both* parents discuss these steps jointly and recognize their importance in contributing to a peaceful bedtime experience.

First, start early. There seems to be a "cut-off" point for Mother when the demands and pressures of the day hit with all their fatiguing impact. Mother is cheerful and fine until a certain time, perhaps, two hours after dinner. Then she finds her patience diminishing rapidly and her irritability level high. Acknowledge this "cut-off" point and make the most of it. Plan to have the children in bed *before* you reach this point of fatigue, for then the child's last memories of Mother are sweet, positive ones, not dark memories of scolding or impatience. Create an after-dinner atmosphere which is a happy one, with parents demonstrating through word and gentle action their love and appreciation for the child. Then the child will drift into slumber with a peaceful smile, not with troubled sobs.

Second, have a consistent bedtime hour, which the child can plan and depend on from night to night. Nature seems to have blessed children with a built-in clock, and when this becomes regulated to a certain hour they look forward to bedtime. But if no designated hour is established and bedtime varies from one to three hours each night, the child fights it regardless of when it finally arrives. Leaving bedtime up for grabs each evening means that things erupt into confusion and frustration for both parent and child. When parents mention "It's time for bed," the child isn't sure they mean what they are saying, and this causes the child to procrastinate or to test and push to the limit.

Too often, this testing goes on for an hour or more, which is very damaging emotionally to all parties involved. So stick to a regular bedtime hour.

Third, establish a quiet time. It is helpful to have the last hour in the day a rather quiet, relaxed time wherein everyone can let down and unwind. Reading or telling stories that are settling and pleasing to children, talking about the good times of the day, or just sitting quietly are conducive to good sleeping habits.

It is the responsibility of the parents to set the stage for bedtime and create the mood. Story time or "talking time" are ideal activities for bedtime preparation. During story time the parent and child are close physically, sitting side by side, or with the child on the parent's lap. Parent and child are also close emotionally, as both are enjoying the calming influence of a quiet activity.

Races, roughhousing and active games are not appropriate to the end of the day. Roughhousing or loud boisterous competition winds little folks up to where sleep is almost impossible. This can cause nightmares and bad dreams. When sleep comes under these conditions, the little bodies are exhausted but the minds are still running at speeds a hundred miles an hour. The results—crying out in their sleep, nightmares, and even sleep-walking for some.

A referral made to me from the medical center illustrates this point. Jerri, eight years old, was being treated by a pediatrician because of her restless sleeping habits. She would wake up in the night crying, talking in her sleep, complaining of seeing monsters, or even occasionally sleep-walking. Medication was not helping her, so she was referred to a counselor for therapy.

A case history taken from the mother and father revealed that Jerri was the youngest of four daughters in the family and the last child. Father had yearned for a son with each pregnancy, only to be disappointed. Finally he concluded that if he could not have a boy, Jerri would fill that need. From the beginning she was dressed like a boy, played mostly with boys in the neighborhood, and her toys were boy oriented—trucks, footballs, and cowboy gear. Father would often play basketball and baseball with her, expecting her to keep up with the boys, or even excel them if she could.

One of the favorite pastimes was to have wrestling matches before bedtime. These would often end up with pillow fights, and sometimes Jerri would end up crying, but Father thought it was great fun. After these competitive games Jerri would fall asleep exhausted, only to wake up two or three hours later with the frightening dreams and sobbing in her sleep. When Father was helped in therapy with his problem, and the family adopted a quiet time for Jerri before going to sleep, her condition began improving and after six weeks had disappeared.

Fourth, plan adequate preparation. Getting ready for bed ought to begin approximately one-half hour before the actual process takes place. The television or stereo should be turned off or the newspaper should be put aside and full attention given to this activity, so that the children fully understand that results are expected. With one eye on television and one eye on the activity of preparing for bed, usually little or nothing happens, except that the parents preach and scold and become emotionally aroused.

The children can sense that there is very little or no follow-through. They sense the parents' lack of commitment to the bedtime preparations, and lacking the initiative or ability to prepare themselves—they naturally stall and put off just as the parent is doing, until an explosion results and everyone is angry.

This fourth step is very necessary, at least in the beginning until a permanent pattern has been established. Further down the road after the pattern has had a chance to jell, the children will be able to do this on their own, but if the foundation is never established clearly the results will be nil.

An important point to remember is to stick to the checklist. If Mother omits or forgets any of the routine happenings such as a drink of water, brushing teeth, offering prayer, telling brother and sister goodnight, it is difficult to stay firm once the child is in bed.

Fifth, bedtime means bedtime! After the routine chores are over and the children are finally in bed, it isn't unusual for the child to test: "Mommy, I forgot to brush my teeth,' or "I want a drink of water,' or "I have to go to the bathroom," or "We forgot to mention Aunt Susie in our prayers." If children soon learn that these excuses are not good enough to warrant getting up again, and that Mother or Father will not indulge them in this kind of play, the testing will phase out. But if parents react to each of the queries, the child is getting mileage out of staying up and the game will continue on his terms.

Even in the unlikely event that something had been overlooked, how tragic would it be to deny a child one of the above privileges? Children are not fragile, they do not shatter, break, or come unglued, as many pseudo-experts in mental health would lead you to believe. Parents made secure with this knowledge can add strength to the child and help him to manage in a more acceptable manner so that everyone can like each other better.

Often the final test for parents is the call, "But I'm not sleepy!" This tempts them more than anything else to give in and allow their child to get up once he is in bed. Parents have often asked me the question, "How can anyone go to sleep unless sleep overtakes them?" or "How can you tell a child to go to sleep and have it happen? You can't push anyone into sleep, it just has to happen."

That is true. You can't wish a person into sleep and have it happen. But you *can* expect that a child stay quietly in bed and not sing, talk to brothers and sisters, play with .toys, or whatever. As silence envelops the child and a quiet atmosphere prevails, sleep follows on its heels. Without the silence or quiet time, sleep has a difficult time in arriving on the scene.

Frequently children have a temporary minor illness, such as a cold or congestion, which awakens them during the night. A child might have a frightening dream which sends him running in to Mother and Daddy to be comforted. This is as it should be on a temporary or momentary basis. Children do need comfort and reassurance during these periods, and parents should provide that kind of assistance when needed. It's when the child carries these patterns of behavior on and on, night after night, and the behavior becomes more intense, that parents should recognize the problem. The child is really crying for help in learning how to cope with darkness, fear, or whatever feelings he manifests.

71

A typical case of this nature existed in the family of a dentist and his wife and their two sons, ages eight and six. It took most of the evening to get the children to bed. They would sleep soundly until about midnight, at which time one of the boys would leave his bed and join the parents. The parents would lie awake waiting for the child to fall asleep so that they could carry him back to his own bed. After settling the one child down, the other would then wake up and take a turn with Mother and Father. This activity would go on through most of the night with first one boy and then the other. By daybreak, everyone was exhausted. The parents felt the need to allow this because each time the children would cry and say that they were frightened to stay in their own beds.

Yes, it is impossible to tell someone he cannot be frightened. But parents *can* comfortably say: "Yes, I know you are frightened of the night voices, or the dark, or the wind outside, but even though they frighten you I think you can stay in your own bed and manage those feelings without taking flight and escaping to Mother and Father."

The parents' sureness about this provides strength for the child to start learning how to cope with his feelings. Helping him work through those feelings provides a deeper love for him than indulging in the interplay of prolonging or putting up with a difficult situation.

Another trying situation can be naptime. Infants sleep most of the time and are awake for short periods.

Gradually this changes to where they are awake more and asleep less. Tiny folk who take naps often fight it unless a routine is established. The same principles used in enforcing the bedtime hour also apply to naptime. The naptime gives needed relief and change to mother and child. Mother can spend her time in other activities, and the child's rest makes him less irritable later.

Many four and five-year-olds slowly wean themselves from a nap in the daytime, and this can be frustrating for the mother as she loses this precious time she once claimed for herself. But even if a child doesn't sleep he can still have a "quiet time" in which he learns to play by himself; or he can even play quietly with other children in the neighborhood. It is important that children not expect Mother to entertain them constantly. This is essential in the child's growing up and freeing himself from such a close involvement with Mother.

Sleeptime, whether it is bedtime or naptime, is an important part of a child's growth. The amount of sleep or quiet time a child has each day can greatly affect the moods of the child and even his health. Thus Mom and Dad must take control for both the child's and the parents' well-being.

How to Live with Your Children and Like Them

Chapter 9

Teaching Character, Ethics, and Morals

The teaching of character, ethics, and morals is too often left to schools, Boy Scout troops, and churches. A majority of parents wish upon their children success and greatness, yet a minority formally teach their children good principles. Many parents even seem oblivious to the importance of teaching high ethical and moral standards. They themselves may not be committed to high moral standards, and thus may lack the ability to provide a strong example and the commitment to instill such values in their offspring.

In teaching principles of ethics, one motto might be, "The younger, the better." It is during *early* childhood that such lessons must be ingrained and good character traits developed. The philosopher Lavater said, "He only is great who has the habits of greatness." And surely the desirable end result can be achieved only if the child has been taught the proper *habits* in his early youth.

Perhaps one of the great gems of wisdom concerning child-rearing comes from a biblical passage—Proverbs 22:6. "Train up a child in the way he should go: and when he is old, he will not depart from it." How meaningful that is in the context of teaching character, ethics and morals!

Parents would do well to remember that a child's growth and development takes shape and form in two areas: 1) physical growth, and 2) emotional maturity. One can grow old in years but remain emotionally immature. Growing old does not automatically mean that a person is emotionally mature.

It is this subject of emotional maturity which has direct relationship to character, ethics, and morality, for it is the teaching of such principles which promotes emotional maturity. Generally a person who does not function upon high moral and ethical standards is emotionally immature. For example, a teenage boy who steals his father's car to satisfy his own whims exhibits selfishness, a form of emotional immaturity. A teenager who indulges in drugs and alcohol to escape reality likewise demonstrates emotional instability and immaturity.

So the natural question is: What criteria can parents use to determine the level of maturity their children possess? Again, we must keep in mind that this knowledge is essential to parents in order to teach the proper standards of character and ethics.

Although there are many measuring sticks that help one judge a person's character and maturity, four basic areas stand out clearly as criteria: 1) How well have they learned to manage feelings and emotions? 2) How well do they manage responsibilities? 3) How well do they manage money? 4) How well do they get along with people?

These areas are "must" factors in a person's finding happiness and hence are vital areas of concern for everyone. Let's explore these four areas in depth and consider their application in child-rearing.

(1) *How well has the young person learned to manage feelings and emotions?*

Does anger, moodiness, jealousy, pouting, depressions, and fear govern him a good deal of the time? Does the child act on impulse, letting go of his actions without considering the consequences, or is he able to conquer and control these feelings when they come along?

To find happiness, people must relate well to other people. We all need status, acceptance, and reassurance from outside relationships. Yet a person who functions on an emotionally immature level brings negative personality traits into a relationship, and sooner or later he will manifest them—selfishness, jealousy, pouting, temper tantrums, and so on. When these problems surface the usual result is the break-up of the relationship. When that happens, the individual causing the problems fails to understand why. He begins to feel that people don't like him, but he can't recognize the reason; so he keeps searching from one relationship to another, always finding failure, frustration, and discouragement.

Usually he develops a poor self-image and even isolates himself from people to avoid further failure experiences. Frequently such persons literally give up the people world. Some go into the drug cult. Other, more intelligent people seek their well-being by desperately immersing themselves in their daily work. Some put extreme efforts into a career, desperately struggling for status and recognition. Whatever the method, they all search for a substitute for people.They end up in a lonely world—loving a piano or a slide rule, or turning to the animal world for love and attention. Often girls become strongly attached to horses or dogs when they are doing poorly in relationships with people.

A teenage boy who had violated the law was incarcerated at the California Youth Authority, an institution where guards rode horses to police the area. The teenager, Joseph, was assigned to groom and care for the horses. When the time arrived for him to be paroled back home to his parents, he could not tear himself from the animals. He wanted to give up his parole. A counseling session with Joseph revealed his feelings.

"Horses will always love you no matter what you do," he said. "They are not moody or selfish, and they do not tell lies. You can depend upon them always being the same. They are better than people, and so I want to stay and be with them."

If parents would teach their children how to manage feelings, control emotions, and establish successful relationships (as discussed in previous chapters), many of these problems and heartaches would be eliminated.

(2) *How well does the young person manage responsibility?*

Strangely enough, the animal and bird species seem to do a better job in teaching their offspring responsibilities than do humans. For instance, prior to laying her eggs, an eagle makes the nest as comfortable as possible, selecting down feathers and the softest, most comfortable materials available for the eggs and baby chicks. Soon after the eggs have hatched and the young fledglings begin to mature, the adult birds begin stripping the nest of all its warmth and comfort. Finally when the new birds are mature enough to fly, there is nothing left of the nest but a few hard rocks and a twig or two. The offspring no longer have a nest to cling to, and the only alternative is to get out and start flying on their own.

Another good example are mother bears, who stay with their cubs about two years. Teaching them to hunt and fare for themselves is a natural schooling almost from the day they are born. When the mother bear feels that the cubs are properly taught and ready to care for themselves, she chases them up a tree and wanders off aimlessly into the forest never to return. The cubs, after many hours of waiting, grow hungry and tired and eventually have to come down and function by themselves.

Many parents lean toward the opposite direction. They often prolong immaturity in their children by taking over and doing tasks for them which in reality are essential for the youngster's growth and normal development. In order to learn, children must be given the opportunity to try. This does not mean that they cannot be supervised or given direction, but when they comprehend and understand they should be allowed to try even though they will make mistakes along the footpath.

Too often, children begin kindergarten without being able to dress themselves. They are poorly toilet trained, and they don't know how to follow directions or complete tasks that are very routine. This is not indicative of their intelligence but rather of their non-involvement in life around them. The simple fact is that if Mother does for them, they do not learn how to do on their own.

Mother's cry is usually, "But Jane is so slow and messy that I can do it for her much faster and with less mess." This is true in the beginning, but if Mother would have patience to teach Jane and then hold her accountable to try, Jane would eventually achieve and both mother and child would be happier and better adjusted.

During early years, children have a driving desire to try. "Let me help! Let me do!" is a familiar plea of pre-schoolers. Yet if parents continue to brush off that plea and squelch the opportunity to try, the child soon learns to sit back and let others do for him. The habit takes root and the pattern continues through adulthood. On the other hand, if the desire to do is encouraged and cultivated, the child will develop positive character traits, ambitions, and confidences which will be typical of him through his life.

Our society has many so-called losers, people who have not learned how to function early in childhood and have continued on unchecked. Being useful, important and needed is important to good mental health, even for children.

The Murphy family was a typical case to illustrate this point. Robert Murphy was a seventeen-year-old junior in high school who was expelled for gambling on campus, failing in school, and having many serious traffic citations, such as drunk driving. Youth authorities came to the school with Robert's parents and asked that Robert be reinstated. A developmental history was taken and some of the following information was obtained.

Mr. Murphy was reared on a dairy farm in the Midwest where he had very little leisure time in his childhood. He had no time for involvement in extra-curricular activities, since he had no time off on the weekends or holidays. Night and morning consisted of chores, and his studies were sandwiched in between.

He had secretly longed for a more balanced and leisurely life, and he felt left out. Nevertheless his years of struggle had developed strong character traits. He had learned to be responsible enough to rise to the level of foreman in his company, where he supervised more than 150 men.

Mrs. Murphy had a similar background. Her mother had been in poor health, and the burden of rearing the family of six children had been placed upon her, the eldest. It was a hard childhood for her, but she developed qualities which enabled her to become a nurse, and at an early age she was promoted to supervisor because of her abilities to lead and direct people competently.

Because of these childhood experiences, both parents were united in wanting more for their children than they each had. They failed to see the good fruits of their childhood struggles—the character traits they had developed. Together, Mr. and Mrs. Murphy devised a plan whereby Robert was given five dollars a day spending money throughout high school, a new car every two years, and an open charge account at the local clothing store. There were no responsibilities or work expected of him because his parents wanted him to have time for all the fun they had missed in their growing-up years.

The results? A high school dropout who was almost a complete failure. During an interview one day, the school counselor learned that Mr. Murphy had damaged a back muscle while mowing the lawn. The counselor queried Robert as to why he did not take over the task to give his father relief. Robert's reply was that he would be embarrassed to have his friends see him working in that manner.

In this case, Robert's parents failed to teach him a principle basic to strong character development—the principle of honest *work*. Many parents have testified that the success of their children in college careers and human relations directly correlates to the ability and opportunity they had to do hard work when they were young. Work is also essential for helping the child feel important to the family. A child that never contributes to the family doesn't really feel he is a part of it. Those who contribute making beds, preparing meals, doing tasks around the house, earning their own money and even giving some of it to other family members—feel that they have a legitimate place in the family and a right to belong.

Herein, then, lies a key to teaching a child responsibility—teaching him to work. Work teaches responsibility; responsibility leads to strong positive character traits; a good character usually means high standards of ethics and morality.

(3) *How well does the child manage money?*

Having children grow up without realizing the value of money can put them at a great disadvantage when the time comes for them to go out into the competitive world. To function successfully as an adult, they must learn the necessity of working and saving for goods and services they desire. The purpose and value of money and how one goes about acquiring money should be taught early in childhood.

The youngster who is carelessly given pennies and dimes "to play with" is missing a great lesson—that real money is not to play with but is to be carefully considered and wisely safeguarded. One mother had repetitive experiences at the grocery store with her child fussing and pleading for something to buy. Since the item was usually not costly, the mother usually purchased the small treat which her child desired.

But the mother found that once the child was in the car he abused or ignored the item he had just been given. A new book ended up crumpled under his feet, or a toy was battered and broken before it arrived home. After many such experiences, the mother finally realized that these free handouts had very little meaning or value to the child once he had received them. So this perceptive mother helped the child make a "store bank." Thereafter, every time the child received a penny for accomplishing some special task he put the money in the "store bank" to save for a treat when Mother again went to the store. If he had not saved enough money, he simply could buy no treat at the store. As this pattern developed, the mother found that the item bought, which the child had earned himself, took on meaning and he appreciated it much more than before.

Another similar situation involved an older child whose parents had done nothing to teach him the ramifications of an allowance. Steve was not taught the art of working to acquire funds and the excitement of buying an item for which he had worked. When Steve arrived at his sixth birthday, the parents announced that he would automatically be given fifty cents a week. They offered no explanation, rhyme or reason behind the handout. They assumed that one of their responsibilities as good parents was to give an allowance to their child.

Steve quickly took the money and was off to the market to spend it. His first purchase was a pair of shoe laces for a man's pair of boots. After that he purchased a package of gum, flavored so hot that he could not chew it. His purchases were of no value and were a waste of his money, but Steve placed no sense of value on the money since he had not worked for it and had not been taught how to manage it and spend it properly. The parents' decision to give this allowance resulted in much frustration both for them and for Steve.

Again, it must be repeated that if a child is to learn the basic principles of money management and appreciation he must be taught methodically just as he would be taught in reading and writing. Parents cannot trust to chance and hope some miracle will do the job for them.

(4) *How well does the child get along with people?*

Getting along with people is not necessarily a trait which comes naturally. It must be learned just like any other character trait. Somewhere in the activities of a child's normal routine, he must be taught by his parents to give and take, to share, and to be kind and considerate.

Amazingly, many children think they can take their half of the pie out of the middle! They have not been taught that most important law of functioning happily in this life—the law of consideration. As inconsiderate children grow into teenagers and then adults, the bulk of their problems stem from that one poison they never learned to flush out—selfishness.

How much safer and happier society would be if more adults had learned in their youth the great destructive results of selfishness!

Another signpost in determining how well a child gets along with people is to observe how confidently he acts with people. Is he basically uncomfortable in a small or large group? Is he ill at ease? Does he phase out or withdraw? Would he rather stay home than relate socially? Or does he converse freely and invest himself in interaction with another person or with a group?

Parents can be valuable aids in helping their children feel comfortable with others by teaching them to relate successfully with other family members and by encouraging appropriate outside friendships.

To sum up, strong character and high ethics and morals are learned and developed during early youth. They are taught most effectively when the parents teach the child four basic principles: 1) how to manage feelings and emotions; 2) how to manage responsibility; 3) how to manage money; and 4) how to get along with people. Once he is successfully functioning in these areas, a child is on the road to achieving attributes of character which will make him of greatest worth to family, friends and society—and to himself.

Chapter 10

Understanding
Feelings

For ages the "generation gap" has been explored and exploited. Therapists have shouted from the housetops the need for parents to communicate with their children. Marriage manuals advise spouses to shout, scream, yell at each other—so long as they communicate.

The art of communication is indeed an area critical to human relationships, and perhaps it can best be described as the art of understanding feelings. For that is what communication is all about.

As we have discussed, the human being is basically a social animal, being at his best when he can relate to other human beings and find comfort, security, reassurance, status, and, most of all, in-depth love. Everyone has moments when the stress and strain of life cause feelings of disappointment, loneliness, fear, or sorrow. Children, like adults, have those days when life becomes difficult. Likewise, everyone has times of excitement, joy, or happiness, and a need to share those times with others.

87

When these needs to share the good or bad creep over us, it's wonderful to have someone with whom we can share deep emotions, someone we can risk letting into our world. What a lonely world it would be if we had to go it alone—always bottle up feelings and keep them to ourselves.

When we are paining emotionally and these feelings get inside, kicking us around, it's difficult to get relief. But if someone would allow us to put these feelings into words, we could spit them out and get rid of the hurt. Just to talk and relate to someone else helps a person to feel better. It's frightening, however, to risk exposing these tender feelings unless we are sure how the other person will respond.

For instance, when a person is experiencing these difficult periods, it is not the proper time for someone else to give advice, to criticize, or to poke fun at the situation, as parents sometimes do. In such situations, too, some parents become anxious as they listen to their child "spouting off," and they turn to anger because they do not know how to cope with what they are hearing.

One of the most discouraging types of communication is to have the listening person phase out—for instance, by reading a newspaper or a book, or even by looking at television—when the troubled person is trying to relate to him. To the troubled person this action means that no one really cares about the dilemma he is in. The child most often reads these actions wrong. He is too young to realize that it isn't that parents do not care, but rather that they do not know how to respond or react to his feelings, so they endeavor to shut them off by turning from the involvement and trying not to hear something they cannot handle.

These communication barriers also go up as parents attempt to discipline a child for misbehavior. Too often, when a child is not performing as parents expect, the tendency is for them to preach and scold about the mistakes. The harping goes on and on. There is very little teaching in this kind of behavior, and as they heap verbal abuse the condition worsens. Jane begins to feel that she is stupid or dumb and really can't perform. She finds herself living the role her parents perceive her as being. Resentment and hopelessness build up until Jane begins functioning in a second-rate manner. If those around her believe she can't manage, she soon begins to believe it herself and gives up trying to manage.

Most of the time parents talk too much in their attempts to change the child's behavior. Verbal communication is fine if it is a constructive process and if all parties involved are willing to use the information brought out as a helpful way to better themselves. But this seldom happens when there is a confrontation and contention. Usually the parties involved use verbalizing as a way of trapping or controlling the other person. Talk, per se, just heats the water; tempers flare, anger erupts, and there is no reasoning or helping each other out of the dilemma.

When Mother makes a statement, "No, you cannot go to Mary's house and play this afternoon," the typical response from her daughter is, "Why can't I go?" As

Mother gives reasons why she should not go, daughter counters with more reasons why she should be allowed to do so, and the debate goes on and on. If only Mother could catch herself when the child asks *why* and explore the *why* out in the open with her daughter!

"Are you asking why, daughter, for *information* or to *trap me into an argument*? If it's for information, I'll give you a brief explanation and that will be the end of the conversation. If you are asking why to develop an argument, forget it, because I'm not going down that footpath. So what will it be?"

Daughter now has to look at the *why* and clarify it for herself as well as for Mother. This takes the steam out of the argument and should settle the problem if Mother will stick to her guns and not be pulled off target. To argue means to clutter the issue.

Many children will follow a parent from room to room to argue their point or to pull the adult off target from the stand he has taken. Again, Mother should take a look at the child's pressing and say: "Why are you pushing or testing? Is it for clarification? Is it because you don't believe I mean what I'm saying? Is it because you think I'll get tired and give in? Could it be because you think you can play on my sympathy and I'll change my mind?" As Mother does this she is not really interested in the child's response, but rather she is doing this to clarify to the child that she knows what is going on.

Teenage children especially find the method of verbally controlling parents very effective in eventually getting their way if they can persist or pursue the argument long enough. Father's nerves will finally tire and he will give in. If Mother or Father would say what they mean and mean what they say the first time around, then walk away from the situation and not pursue it on and on verbally, the child would not have anyone to battle with.

In this day and age all a child needs to say is, "My parents won't communicate with me," and for some foolish reason this statement cuts Mother to the quick. She will do anything rather than be accused of this. When the child makes that statement, what she really means is, "My parents won't give me my own way" or "They won't listen to me." Of course, the child feels that to have parents listen to her means that they will agree to let her do as she pleases.

It is most difficult to listen when a child is angrily accusing us of wrongdoing. "Mother, I think you are a so-and-so," or "I don't think you love me," or "I don't believe you are honest." To hear these accusations hurts and puts one on the defensive. When this happens, our ability to listen goes out the window and we find ourselves proving or debating that what we are being accused of is not true. As we start defending or proving, the child is blocked from getting his feeling up and out. Shutting him off and pushing him back does not help him get rid of the feeling. Parents must remember that children often say things they don't really mean when angry. After the smoke has cleared, they feel sorry for what they said.

It is not necessary for parents to defend or prove themselves. How much better it would be if the parent could keep his feet on the ground and not react or interact except to encourage the child to explore more deeply the things she is saying. This certainly does not mean that a parent has to agree with what the child is saying, but he can listen and let her get it off her chest. As Julie talks long enough and does not have a partner to fight with she will gradually come down to earth and put herself together and, best of all, feel better. After the anger and resentment have been drained off, more sensible verbalization will take its place and good feelings of caring will develop.

To reiterate, if parents will not react or interact to what they are hearing, but rather just *actively listen* and encourage the child to get the emotions out, the parents can act as an anchor post for the child to tie to during the storm. The parents then act as a catalyst to dissolve the hurt or pain. After all, there are times when a youngster has a genuine need to talk and the right to be listened to, in depth, without a power struggle erupting between parent and child.

When the child is under emotional stress, parents do not have to know the *answers* or go out and be a *fix-it person* for the child. Rather they need to be a listener so that the child feels that someone cares. That is the most important service the parent can perform at that moment. When children do not get this kind of support from parents, they finally close the door and won't let anyone into their world. It hurts too much to expose one's self only to be shot down verbally.

A quiet, withdrawn adult is basically one who never was taught the art of relating to others on a feeling level as a child. The basis for so many marital problems is that adults have difficulty in loving each other on a feeling level because they were not exposed to this kind of a relationship as a child in the family environment. The physical aspect of the body cries out for a relationship with people, but the psychological make-up puts the brakes on and will not allow the dormant feelings to emerge.

People must get their well-being from somewhere, and if they have failed in relating to humans they are prone to stop investing love because it hurts too much. They then throw all their efforts into material things of the world in the search for acceptance. They might have an intense drive for wealth, knowledge, music or art abilities. Many of the so-called intellectuals are deeply troubled people who have failed in social relationships time and time again and finally, in frustration, look to other fields of endeavor for status. This is why they invest so heavily of their time and talents in the arts, science, or whatever—they are filling up the void they experience in their poor relationships with people. At best, however, material achievement is a poor substitute for social human relationships. It's very hard to love in depth a test tube, a sheet of music, or a slide rule. But these substitutes are better than nothing, and some people push their abilities to great heights in such areas.

I saw a brilliant law student, Harry, in therapy for more than a nine-month period. In the beginning he was very angry and defiant in regards to his relationship with people. He was always alone and spent most of his waking hours in deep study, seeking knowledge vehemently. He disliked his mother, his father, his sister, his grandmother, the girl he sat next to in class, and so on.

During one session, he expressed the wish to do research for a prominent law firm in the Bay area and wondered how he might gain employment with them. We thought for a moment, and then he came up with an idea that perhaps the firm would be impressed with his ability to master law if he were to memorize one of his textbooks. The book he indicated contained over a thousand pages of law materials. The thought of memorizing it seemed overwhelming to me, and I asked him how long it would take to master the text. The answer was almost frightening. Harry felt that if he read it over twice, or maybe three times, he could memorize it verbatim. The next question was, "When can you be finished?" Harry thought that over the weekend would be sufficient time.

As Harry remained in therapy, he gradually resolved the feelings of mistrust, anger and fear about people which he had acquired through the years. He learned how to cope with mother, father and grandmother openly and honestly. In the past, his method of surviving had been to get angry in their presence and withdraw.

It was a red-letter day when Harry came to the office and happily told me that he had risked signing up as a prop man for a stage play on campus and had gotten the job. Here he became a part of the human race again. He was needed, and the people in the production liked him enough to include him for snacks after rehearsals. Harry was on the mend now, and he could strike up conversations and include people in his thoughts without becoming so anxious and self-conscious. One girl in particular he liked, but had not advanced enough emotionally to assume an in-depth relationship.

Towards the end of therapy, Harry looked and felt much better about himself as a person. Then one day, with a big smile he announced that he was giving up law. He saw it as a waste of time and was going to take a salesman's job, he said. I asked why he had made such a big and abrupt decision. His answer came quickly and forthrightly: The only reason he had studied law was to find legal ways to fight people he didn't like. He was liking people now, and he found that they were liking him, so he didn't have to fight anymore. He concluded that it was better to get along with people than to fight them all the time.

So let's not fight our children or have them fight us. In parent-child relationships the art of communicating, of understanding feelings, is vital to the child's growth and to family harmony. As parents listen unemotionally to their children and allow them the chance to *feel* and express feelings verbally, they will find themselves contributing valuably to their children's well-being. The children in turn will feel an acceptance, love, and concern which will carry through and make great impact on their adult lives.

Chapter 11
Bedwetting

For some families there is nothing that causes more discouragement, resentment, and perplexity than the problem of bedwetting, or enuresis (en-yoo-*ree*-sis), as it is medically labeled. Through the years, many gimmicks have been created and employed to cope with this problem.

Some families impose a thirst ban on the child, precluding him from having water or liquids after a certain hour in the evening. Others have established a "guard-duty" system wherein one of the parents makes the rounds every few hours during the night and wrestles the children out for toilet chores.

Perhaps the epitome of gimmicks is the rubber sheet which boasts a metal plate underneath connected to an electrical current. When the drops of urine hit the mat, an electrical charge sets off a bright light and a hodge-podge of noise sufficient to cause a mild heart attack. But for all the ingenuity expended, such gimmicks are frustrated efforts which don't solve the problem.

We even hear of physical abuses as a means to cure enuresis—making the child sleep in smelly sheets for long periods of time; requiring small tots to launder the soiled bed-clothing; or heaping on ridicule, shame, or constant preaching and scolding.

Often we see bedwetting going from one generation to another. In therapy we usually find that a child's parent or close relative had the same condition during his juvenile years.

Thus surfaces the common belief that the bed-wetting problem is an inherited, physiological problem which children cannot help. However, 98 percent of the enuresis cases seen in therapy in our clinic over the last ten years have not had physical implications but emotional and psychological ones. Eighteen percent of the emotionally disturbed children seen in therapy from ages five to ten years had a problem of bed-wetting which plagued the home. For ages five to eleven years the percentage dropped to 5 percent, and for eleven to eighteen years it dipped to 2 percent.

Nevertheless it is advisable for parents who question the source of the problem to schedule a medical checkup to relieve any uncertain feelings about the child's physical condition. In this chapter we will deal with enuresis as an emotional problem, since that is most often the case.

In spite of all the ramifications of bedwetting, with all its "helpful" gimmicks, the big factor which stands in the way of solving the problem is Mom and Dad.

They tend to take the "monkey" into their own laps rather than making the child "own up" to the problem.

As parents and child come for therapy, then, my first step is to work with the parents, to provide them with the insight and understanding necessary to cure the problem. As they begin to see what is really taking place, it is amazing how quickly the problem clears up.

Most parents fail to understand one simple concept—that nature sends signals to everyone, whether it is a child of five or an adult of fifty. When it's time to urinate, signals are sent and received by the brain whether people are asleep or awake. Even in deep sleep adults pick up signals of the need to urinate, and they wake up and relieve themselves. And children receive the signals in exactly the same way.

The bedwetter is basically the one who chooses to *ignore* the clear signals he receives while he is asleep. Consequently he lets go without considering the responsibilities or consequences. As this continues, it develops into a lackadaisical habit which will continue if the child does not have the reassuring support from parents that it can stop. One of the first defenses a bedwetting child makes is that he cannot help it, that he is not aware of the bedwetting when he is asleep. And herein lies the basis for bedwetting—the fact that children convince parents that they are not capable of being in control of this condition. If parents buy this story they will not be able to provide the support necessary for the child to change. They will excuse or accept this behavior without really trying to correct it.

It is important to know that children do not like functioning in this manner. The shame and ridicule heaped upon them is very damaging to their self-image. They see themselves as failures and worry much of the time, especially as bedtime approaches. This closes the door for them to have friends over to sleep or to accept invitations to slumber parties outside the family unit. A child in this dilemma tries to hide the problem by stashing soiled pajamas or under-clothing away in a dark closet or drawer, hoping that no one will notice the accident. The child is tense, yet on his own he is not strong or mature enough to set guidelines or limits for himself.

How, then, does a parent provide the support necessary to help his child stop bedwetting? What do we mean by "support"?

First, as we have discussed, it is essential for the parent to acknowledge that a child as well as an adult receives warning signals.

Second, from this knowledge comes confidence which enables the parent to take a firm stand, being sure of himself. To offer support, the parent must verbally communicate the confidence and expectation that the child *does* have the ability to stop bedwetting. For example, a typical conversation might go: "Jimmy, this bedwetting must stop and you *can* stop it. Now, I will do whatever I have to in order to help you stop it. What should I do… get angry or bench you? I'd rather not do this, but if you do not take control of yourself, I will have to take control for you."

If the parent decides to bench the child, when the child awakens with a wet bed he immediately goes on the bench or in the time-out room until he commits himself not to wet the bed. If he wets the bed again after making his commitment, the parent might say: "Now you said you wouldn't and you have. Do you need to spend more time on the bench until you can prove you will do what you say?"

The all-important point to remember is that this dialogue and approach must be supportive, not punitive. As the child learns that the parent means business and is convinced that the child can succeed, he will begin to respond and control himself. The child needs the sureness and confidence of the adults and family, but he needs someone to set limits and hold him accountable for his actions. When the parent is sure that Jimmy can manage this problem, Jimmy feels the strength and begins to be a believer himself.

Parents should keep in mind that children do not change completely overnight. They do change by degrees. For instance, in the beginning Jimmy will stay dry one night out of four; whereas in the past he was wet every night for years. From this glimmer of hope the parents gain new strength. The pattern might change to one dry night and one wet night, but soon there will be more dry nights than wet. It will be a delight to see Jimmy go dry an entire week, then two weeks, then a month, until the wetting finally phases out entirely. What a relief it is for Jimmy to have this condition off his back and be through with it for good!

A word of caution here. When Jimmy starts to improve, the family becomes so delighted that they tend to over-praise and reward at the signs of a little improvement. If they do this, Jimmy will mistake the praise as a sign that the little improvement is good enough and will stop trying, thinking that he has arrived at his destination and can let down. Too much rewarding or praising can be damaging to his progress and he will revert back to the old way. Staying dry is a normal procedure for all children, and his accomplishments should be treated as normal without a lot of fanfare or applauding from the sidelines.

Is it necessary then for bedwetting to be such a nightmare? Why should parents become trapped in this age-old problem? The springed coil which hinders parents from helping their children is the dilemma of not being sure of what to do or feeling sorry for the child. These are the feelings which prolong the problem. During World War II, when so many young males were drafted into the service, too many were caught up in the trauma of bedwetting even at age eighteen.

A young lady, eighteen years old, came to me in despair. She was soon to be married and was haunted with fear because of her struggle with enuresis. This had been her constant battle through life. She had tried all the gimmicks and pursued all avenues known to her with no success. Her opening question was, "Should I give up the young man and a chance for marriage?" To be embarrassed by sharing this problem with someone she loved was too much.

I helped her understand that she was really no different from other human beings and her feelings were normal. As I convinced her that her feelings could be controlled and governed just as stealing, overeating, or losing one's temper could be controlled, she steadily improved. Having problems and then feeling too overwhelmed to cope with them is very frightening. But when a person can get understanding, strength, and support from someone else in working through a trauma, it can be resolved much more easily and permanently.

Melvin, age fourteen, had had enuresis all his life, and his parents had given up hope that his condition would ever be corrected. A neighbor lady told the family she had received professional help for her daughter. Desperately they asked for therapy, but they were very skeptical of much success.

Schools had complained of the odor in the classroom; Melvin's peers made fun of him and would hold their noses in his presence; most of the time he was a loner, and when he did play it was mostly with smaller children. In therapy, the mother said she was sure Melvin had inherited this weakness from her mother's side of the family. She counted on her fingers how many relatives were victims of the same malady.

The father came to the fourth session, announcing that he would have to skip the fifth session a week hence because it was time for his annual deer hunt. He also said it was harder getting away this time, as Melvin wanted to be included in the outing. Of course, Melvin could not possibly go. They could not have a boy in camp who wet the bed, as there were no facilities to launder or dry out the sleeping bag.

Melvin spoke up and said, "If you let me go, I'll stay dry and won't be any trouble."

Father looked mildly surprised. "How could that be? You have wet the bed every night since you were a baby. I'd have to break camp and bring you home after the first night. We would miss all the fun."

Melvin continued to beg so much for a chance that I explored his statement. "Why do you feel you can refrain from wetting during the hunt?"

"I want to go so badly that I'll do anything for a chance," came the answer.

If Melvin could go and not wet the bed, would he be acceptable? Father thought for a time and then said: "You are sure asking a lot from me. This is my only vacation for the year. He could spoil it the first night. If he did, I'd turn right around and bring him home."

I asked, "Would it be worth a try?"

Melvin, his mother and I thought it would, and the father finally agreed. But he warned, "The first time he slips I'll ship him off back home."

Two weeks later in therapy there was an accounting for what had happened. Father grinned. "Could you imagine?" he asked. "Melvin stayed dry every night till the last one prior to coming home."

This gave the parents enough insight to see that when situations were important enough Melvin could control himself like anyone else. From that incident they could see that Melvin's plight was not as hopeless as he had led them to believe. Within two months his enuresis was under control permanently.

Nancy, age ten, was experiencing difficulty in this area. When confronted by her parents she would cry and shake uncontrollably, accusing them of not being understanding.

"If you loved me and cared about my feelings you would not say anything, since I can't help bedwetting," was her typical complaint. This was frightening to the parents, so they tried to live with the problem. Every few days, however, their displeasure and anger would well up and they would preach, scold and pick again. No worthwhile results were accomplished, and the family became caught up in a vicious circle.

Nancy came to one of her therapy sessions excited about going to visit Grandmother for ten days during summer vacation. She talked incessantly of the good times they would have together, going shopping, swimming at the beach, taking picnic lunches to the zoo, and so on. I listened and then, to bring her back to reality, wondered what she would do about her bedwetting problem at Grandmother's. Nancy stopped, thought, and almost as though she were talking to herself, shook her head and said slowly, "No, that would not do at Grandmother's."

I questioned, "Why?"

"Well," said Nancy, "Grandmother is very particular about her house and what people do there and she would not like that to happen." Then she sighed wistfully, clasped her hands together and said, "I'll have to stop when I go to her place. I always want her to like me." Grandmother was more meaningful to her than her own parents and Nancy was content to present a good image to her.

There are numerous examples in which a child has wanted certain things enough to stop bedwetting in order to have his desires fulfilled. Being given new underwear with the condition that it would be taken back if soiled; getting a new bed with pretty coverings; being allowed to have a friend sleep over—these and many other worthwhile experiences have been factors in helping a child take control of enuresis. They further prove the point that if the child is of average physical and mental health and receives support and strength from parents he can manage to conquer bedwetting.

Chapter 12

Drugs and Alcohol

A newspaper published a photo of a demolished motorcycle that had carried a teenage youth to his death by plunging through the guard rail of the highway and striking a tree. The story that accompanied the photo told of Billy N. being under the influence of drugs when the accident happened and listed drugs as the cause of death.

The need for such drugs as narcotics (heroin, etc.) has been one of the major reasons for burglaries, rapes, and even murders. A user keeps hustling during his waking hours to find enough finances to buy a "fix." The longer the user goes without a fix, the more desperate he becomes. During this condition of desperation, he will resort to almost any means to satisfy his craving. The addiction becomes so great that he can use the same dosage a normal person would use for major surgery. Thus, much of his normal body functioning stops, with the exception of the heart and lungs, and goes into a kind of "deep freeze." When the drug wears off and the body comes back to near normal, he feels a good deal of pain, especially in the nerve endings that are awakened from the deep sleep. People smoking marijuana do not receive these traumatic experiences nor is there a hangover effect such as alcoholics experience. Alcoholism also poses a grave danger to society. Every year alcoholics and heavy drinkers contribute greatly to the death rate in automobile accidents, home fires, and other tragedies.

Over the years we have learned that drug and alcohol abuse among adolescents can be found in almost any family. All parents need to be aware of a few very important facts. These include: how to recognize substance abuse, what they should do if they find that their child is experimenting with drugs or alcohol, and some of the effective methods for treatment.

How to Recognize the Problem

Often the parents seem to be the last ones to know. The easiest way to be certain is to do a urine analysis for drugs and alcohol, using one of several methods. Parents can request to have it done at any medical lab, although some states require the parents to secure a physician's order. Parents can buy "over-the-counter" drug screen kits that test for different drugs, such as alcohol, marijuana, cocaine, nicotine, opiates, and amphetamines. These tests are not as accurate as those done at a lab are, but they have fairly accurate results and are less expensive. Also, parents may call their local health units to see if there are community programs in their area that offer "free" drug screen tests.

A less reliable method of drug "testing" is for parents to watch for major changes in their children's behavior or in the type of friends they have—changes in their choice of friends, in their school grades, in their eating and sleeping patterns, and in the ways in which they spend their free time.

The least reliable method of determining if adolescents are involved with drugs or alcohol is to ask them. Even though this may work in a few cases, the vast majority of teenagers will lie about their substance abuse. Often, adolescents claim to be telling the truth, because in their minds, they are not "doing" drugs or alcohol if they have had none within the last three days.

Many professionals routinely require a urine analysis for any adolescent whose parents suspect drug use. When young people accuse their parents, therapist, or probation officer of not trusting them after they have denied substance abuse, the adults could respond, "This test is to protect you. If it is negative, you can hold it up to the whole world as proof that you are not using drugs. You see, we are on your side. If you tell us that you are not using anything, we want to help you prove it." This takes the guesswork and arguing out of the suspicion and allows the teenager one last chance to be honest. If the test is negative, congratulate the child and turn your attention toward any of their other concerns, such as low school grades, curfew hours, arguing, lack of friends, etc. If the test is positive, we know that we must first deal with the substance abuse problem before we can effectively help with other problems.

Initial Strategies

What must parents do once they know there is a problem with drug abuse? It is our opinion that a problem exists when any child has abused drugs at least once. Even though there are some basic elements of treatment, every case must be individualized for each young person and his or her family. Some adolescents need several months of inpatient treatment, followed by several years of outpatient treatment. In these cases, stronger and more defined controls must be employed to help the teenagers until they and their parents have the strength to be less restricted and yet drug free.

Many parents ask how they should react when their son or daughter comes home drunk or on drugs the *first time*. They ask, "Should we put our arms around him and tell him that we love him? Should we just ignore the whole thing and hope it was a single event, or what?" Based on experience and research, the most effective method of dealing with a teenager is to be very stern *the very first time*. Let your child know that you are upset, disappointed, and very serious about stopping the problem.

The "stern and strict" method works. When parents "ignore and hug" their child, they do so with their feelings and emotions. If children experience a positive or neutral feeling from their families, with no uncomfortable consequences, they are much more likely to see drugs or alcohol in a positive light and will continue in the use. If their initial experience is paired with a negative light, they will refrain from future use. Many teenagers have reported that they went out and got drunk a second and third time because they really believed their parents did not seem to mind. But, several adolescents said they stopped drinking after the initial experience because of the strong emotional reaction of their family, coupled with strong consequences. Parents' negative emotions and stern consequences protect their children from future harm.

Consequences

What consequences are effective? Most parents "ground" their teenagers to the house as a consequence when they catch them abusing alcohol or drugs. Our experience is that this method is not effective. When teenagers are grounded to the house, very little teaching of correct behavior is done, and the whole family tends to suffer by having an angry teenager "caged up" in the house. Instead, we recommend a much more effective technique, which we call "grounding teenagers to adult supervision." This means that the teenager can go anywhere he wants or needs to--shopping at the mall, football games, dances, movies, etc., as long as a parent or other *responsible* adult is at all times within fifty feet of them. As long as the child is doing well, the parent does not need to talk or interact with the child, but must be nearby to watch him.

If teenagers say, "You don't trust me," agree with them. Say something like, "If I could really trust you,

you would not have started drinking or using drugs in the first place." Sometimes they will say, "Okay, I'll just stay home and go nowhere." In that case, say, "Fine. Stay home. Just remember that it is is your choice to go or stay, not mine. But if you do go, I'll be nearby. Either way, the teenager is under the supervision of his or her parents. If it is impossible for a parent to go with the teenager, then choose carefully another responsible adult to be there. The point is that he does not go anywhere alone. He needs supervision. He must therefore behave differently; and the parents will begin to learn much more about him and his friends without having conflict. This method has been used for over twenty years and it has helped the great majority of families. Granted, it can be inconvenient for the parents, because it will disrupt their schedule for a few weeks or months, but the positive changes are more than worth it.

A police officer and his wife came to therapy because their teenage daughter was drinking alcohol with her friends every Friday or Saturday night. They had tried grounding her and taking away privileges. When her grounding time was finished, she would return to the same friends and drink again. When the parents told her that she could now go anywhere she wanted to, as long as her mother or father was nearby, things started to improve. She went to all of the high school football games and dances. Her parents volunteered to be chaperones. They stayed near her, but kept a "low profile." Soon Melissa discovered that she had more fun being sober than when drinking. She began to make new friends who did not drink. After four or five weeks, the parents let her have some of her independence *a little at a time.*

In a more serious case, a couple actually attended school with their fifteen-year-old son because he was using drugs at school. After three weeks of this, the parents were able to stay home and let the teachers help by escorting him to and from classes. The parents continued to pick him up from school at the end of the school day. This was a major inconvenience for the parents because each of them had a job, but the results were spectacular. Within two months, he was allowed to go alone for short periods of time and to lengthen the time between counseling visits. Six months after the last therapy sessions, this young man phoned in to report that things were still going well. He finished the conversation by saying, "I want to thank you for helping my parents." The message was loud and clear. He really did appreciate his parent's involvement, even though at first he denied this.

When ending the "grounding to parents" the teenager should be given independence gradually. For example, after a few weeks, the child could go to a friend's home if the parents are at home and can be trusted. The next week they could allow a little more freedom. If the child backslides, the parents must start over again for two or three weeks and then try giving

113

freedom again. This procedure may have to be repeated until the teenager really decides to change.

Therapy

Choose a therapist who understand drug abuse and has experience working with parents. During outpatient therapy, cover three main areas:

(1) Identify and treat the stressors in the teenager's life, such as peers, academic problems, and sibling rivalry.

(2) Identify and treat common adolescent mental problems, such as anxiety, depression, and attention deficit/hyperactivity disorder.

(3) Identify and teach teenagers how to avoid environmental triggers that can cause a craving for alcohol or drugs, such as being with certain friends or in certain homes or businesses where drugs and alcohol are freely served.

Conclusion

Let's return to the newspaper article mentioned at the beginning of this chapter; Billy, whose problem finally caused his violent death. Those who knew Billy saw him with his mother and father in therapy sporadically through the years. His close friends knew that the drug problem had come as an aftermath of trouble that he had experienced throughout his life. When Billy was young, he was quiet and withdrawn. He had a poor self-image and would not risk investing in people or things. Gradually his personality changed and he became bold, angry, and defiant. During the last year of his life, Billy was involved in many crises. He had dropped from the football team, failed a semester of school, lost his part-time job, and had to be removed from home because of the turmoil he had created in each of the situations. His mother and father did not stay in therapy consistently enough to be successful, and Billy was constantly filled with resentment, anger, failure, and hopelessness. He felt the only way he could find relief from these heavy feelings was to use drugs. He even admitted that under the influence of drugs he could take a trip over the rainbow and stay until his money ran out. It's no wonder Billy hated to come back to the atmosphere he had created in the real world. He didn't like himself as a person or the way he functioned; but, right or wrong, he was functioning in the only way he had learned. By himself, he wasn't strong enough to change.

So it is with people using alcohol or drugs constantly. To a degree, these crutches provide temporary relief to a troubled mind. To take those crutches away from a person without helping him learn how to cope with his real problems of stress is not a lasting solution. If parents will take an active role in the treatment of substance abuse, and if they can find an experienced substance abuse counselor, in most cases, they can be successful before the problem becomes severe.

How to Live with Your Children and Like Them

Chapter 13

The Challenge of Television, Video Games, Movies, and the Internet

During the last few decades, nothing has rated so high on popularity polls as movies and television for sources of entertainment. For years, adults as well as children have flocked to the movie theater or TV room as a diversion from daily routines and rigors. One of the major reasons for the popularity of such entertainment media is that they provide escape from the real world into a world of pretend, or of vicariously living through someone else. This escape can at times be beneficial. The struggle of life for all of us becomes perplexing on occasions, at times even overwhelming. These periods are like carrying a pail of water along a difficult pathway. When we first start out with the pail, even though it's full, we manage it quite well because we are rested and our strength has not been expended. The further we carry the pail, the more energy we use up, until finally our strength is gone and we are exhausted. If at that point we would put down the pail and walk

117

away from it for a rest, our strength would return and replenish so that we could pick up the pail once more and move forward with ease. If we didn't take time out to gain back the energy needed, the load would be so heavy that we would not be able to manage it and we would give up. By recognizing our fatigue at certain intervals and taking a rest period, we can survive the ordeal and carry on quite well.

Media diversions provide a rest stop for many people wherein they escape from the heavy loads they are carrying. To daydream, fantasize, and live vicariously through the success, thrills and excitement of someone else's experience gives a needed change of pace. Such diversions take a person out of a world of heartaches and into another world where he can place himself in a more romantic or carefree role, living the part of the hero in each adventure portrayed. Under this hypnotic spell, a person's problems can't get to him. This accounts for the fact that a depressed or troubled housewife spends much of her time reading books or watching television. The casual observer would think she is lazy and avoids work. In reality she is escaping from her problems because they hurt too much.

There seems to be three basic positions that people in general tend to drift to in regard to watching television and other related diversions:

(1) *Television is taboo!*

These families can see no good in television. Time spent in viewing the "boob tube" is a total waste and nothing productive can come from it. In fact, it can be damaging.

People in this category attempt to fill that time slot with music, dance, or education for their children, or some form of family activity instead. To this group, television is a kind of dirty word and should be avoided at all costs.

(1) *Television or die!*

This group catches a large majority of our population and consists of people who turn on the television as the first ritual they perform in the morning and run it constantly until the last family member falls asleep at night. For so many of these people, television is like a chum or old friend keeping them company. Without television they become lonely and depressed. It stays on continually as a companion, regardless of the program or entertainment aired.

(3) *Television with prudence.*

This category is a happy medium between the other two extremes, and consists of people who deliberately select and choose programs which meet the standards they emulate or want to achieve. These people plan ahead, research the TV or movie guide, and evaluate the type of program to be aired. They reject programs that are substandard by turning off the set and leaving it idle, moving on to family-made activities or projects that are more meaningful. They have unusual self-discipline.

In each of these three groups are people who vehemently defend their positions. However, group two, "Television or die!" perhaps has the weakest position. A discussion of the fallacies and harm in this approach would be needless. Judgment on the other two categories may not be so clear. Let's critique for a moment the "Television is taboo!" approach.

In some ways this philosophy is sad because there are many programs which can create learning, broaden one's understanding of the world we live in, encourage an appreciation for the arts, and provide worthwhile temporary diversion from life. It is not feasible to shut out the world around us. If we are to survive we must be generally knowledgeable in many areas, knowing good from evil, bitter and sweet, sadness and joy. We cannot close our door to the world and be fearful to live.

This group can argue, and rightly so, that there is so much "trash" being viewed on television that they do not want their children exposed to the propaganda—the deceitful commercial advertising, the products promoted, the materialistic emphasis, and so on. Children cannot walk through life without encountering this situation at some time, however, and parents should teach children at an early age how to evaluate and cope with substandard principles running rampant around them. A great deal of teaching can take place as parents help them select proper programs and entertainment which will adhere to the standards of the family. To rule out media diversions completely, as being bad would be like saying we should never fly in airplanes because some of them crash. True, some of them do crash, but in general the airplane has brought added blessings into our lives.

The third group, "Television with prudence," is probably the one which is most compatible with well-adjusted lives. A mature, well-disciplined person can get the best of both worlds by exercising this selective control.

If more people would be selective and reject the trash that comes across the air waves, without rejecting the whole medium, the companies would very soon clean up the things which frustrate and embarrass viewers. We hear of much organized effort by society to control food prices and get rid of inferior merchandise, yet why have we not used this type of community pressure to boycott inferior movies and television shows which tear down the morals of our society? If an organized effort would be forthcoming to review programs prior to their public showing and, if they were found distasteful, to mount group pressure to reject them, the quality of entertainment would be quickly improved.

Children are the most precious commodities in life, yet parents allow them to absorb the sick and decayed moral standards of society. It is no wonder some tend to adopt these lifestyles as their own. No one can be exposed constantly to violence, drug abuse, immoral sex activities, dishonesty, distortions, and perversions without having these impressions rub off little by little on their thinking.

Research clearly indicates that if the human mind is brainwashed or whitewashed over long periods of time with the same propaganda over and over again it begins to think and function along those same lines. In the beginning one might abhor the ideas, but then resistance to them deteriorates and breaks down. Erosion sets in, and soon a person begins acting as he is thinking. If negative thoughts are involved, there can be trouble. Society has the power and weapons to combat this type of propaganda that is camouflaged as entertainment, if people, especially parents, would unite and make known what is acceptable to them and what is not.

This gets us back to the basic premise and the major reason why media diversions have such a magnetic appeal. To reiterate, the appeal comes because the media helps people to escape into the world of pretend or make-believe where they can live vicariously through someone else. To have a place where one can go to find relief and replenishment is fine. The problems result when one goes there too often and stays too long. Then the "escape hatch" can interfere with learning how to function in the real world. Children who spend too much time with the media do not learn how to cope in real life with peers, problems, and live situations around them.

There has never been a period of time in America when children are more knowledgeable than now. Likewise, there has never been a period of time when wisdom has been so lacking in their make-up. This is because they are so lacking in real-life experiences. Their only method of learning is to live vicariously through make-believe or pretend situations that all too often are not meaningful enough to prepare them for life. Their minds become lazy as they allow someone else to do their thinking and reacting. They squelch creative potentials by diverting their time from hand projects and reading to sitting and watching. They weaken their minds, creatively and intellectually, and weaken their bodies physically.

Thus the entertainment media do indeed pose a challenge—yet one which parents *must* meet full strength as they teach the principle of prudence to their children and exemplify it themselves.

How to Live with Your Children and Like Them

Chapter 14

Poor Eating Habits

Nothing in child rearing seems to cause more worry to a mother than the food intake and proper diet of her child. Obese adults can often trace their problems back to the trend of stuffing or overeating due to the constant urging of parents to clean up their plates or take double portions of food to "keep up their strength." Too often the supposed criterion for staying well and healthy is to develop big appetites. Some mothers think food is a cure-all for all ills.

One mother with a troubled daughter thought that the way to comfort or reassure her was to bake goodies or cakes for her. She thought that food might make her feel better when the going was tough. The daughter, now an adult, weighs nearly three hundred pounds. Her weight problem started at age four.

The other extreme to this dilemma is the problem of children who are very "picky" eaters. If this problems occurs consistently, the wise mother should arrange a medical checkup to make sure that there are no physical problems connected with poor eating habits. If the child receives a clean bill of health, there are other factors to explore.

Mealtime should be a pleasurable experience wherein the family can come together in a quiet, relaxed atmosphere to enjoy one another's companionship. It should be a time when family members can share pleasant experiences, and find reassurance and acceptance. Good and pleasurable food is comforting and in normal situations tends to enhance the well-being of the eaters. Thus this hour should be the highlight of the day for family members.

The pleasant experience of mealtime, however, can be turned into an emotional fiasco if one or more of the children chooses to play or dawdle with the food placed before them. Ofttimes it's the skinny child who eats less at mealtime, causing the parents to feel that he is undernourished and therefore must eat to stay healthy. The parents become anxious and resort to pressuring by preaching, scolding, threatening, bribing, and playing games with him as a means to get him to eat. Some children will store the food up in their cheeks and not swallow, thus exasperating the parents. Mother or father will sometimes assume the duty of shoveling the food in for their children, so a power struggle develops. The dinner hour goes on and on, filled with emotional disturbance that no one enjoys. Usually each member leaves the table angry with the others.

The fact is that the child does not exist who would starve himself when there is good food around. Simply stated, when a child is hungry he will eat. When he is not hungry and his appetite has been satisfied he will not eat. The law is simple: You can put a child in front of food but you cannot force him to eat. One of the biggest hindrances to proper eating is too many snacks available during the day. With snacks the child can pick and choose the foods to suit his taste, whether they are good for him or not. When his appetite has been satisfied with snacks, he comes to the table not hungry. The tummy is full. His wants for food have been satisfied, so all the anger, coaxing, or playing games to encourage eating is useless. Without being aware of what they are doing, parents undermine the mealtime by providing snacks all through the day. Some children can handle both snacks and meals together, and one will not interfere with the other, but most children cannot. If the child can handle both, snacks should be allowed. If not, the snacks should be eliminated, at least until the need for more food increases.

At mealtime, the parent should put small portions of food on the child's plate, letting the child ask for more. Frequently, loading the plate heavily will take the appetite away and discourage the child. After placing the food on the plates in small portions, no more preaching, scolding or game-playing should be allowed. Should the child dawdle, daydream, or put off the task of eating, the parents should ignore the behavior and continue on with their own meal. When the parents have finished, the table should be cleared of food and dishes, that being the end of the meal regardless of how much the child has eaten or how much protest of hunger the child voices.

The next step is not to allow any more snacks or food until the next meal. The child may hold out for one or two meals, but when his hunger increases he will eat at mealtime.

If the parents will be consistent, the eating habit pattern can be changed to a pleasant, delightful and healthy experience for the child. It's interesting to note that poor eating habits seldom occur in large families. In this situation, each child must hurry to get his share of the food and is stimulated to eat from seeing others eat all around him.

It's reassuring for Mother to realize that children's appetites, like adults, vary as to the amount and kind of food they desire. If Mother keeps a record over a given period (a week), she will find that her child has acquired a fairly well-balanced diet, even though one day he will feast on carrots, avoiding most other things, and the next day change to milk, and so on.

Controlling Behavior at Mealtime

It is most important to expect control at the dinner table. If Elizabeth is disruptive at mealtime and out of control to the point where it interferes with the rapport of the family, she should be benched or sent to a time-out place until she can put herself together emotionally before returning to the meal. (Refer to Chapter 2 for more detail.)

There should be an orderly, consistent pattern of mealtimes, meals being served at approximately the same hour each day. This regularity will serve to eliminate snacks. For instance, if dinner is normally served at 6:00 P.M. and is held off at times for Daddy who arrives at 8:30 P.M., the children become too tired and hungry. There is a built-in need for snacks to tide them over, and mealtime then becomes a fizzle. If Father cannot be home at 6:00 P.M. or the regular dinner hour, he should instruct the family to proceed without him. Adults can adjust to the change better than children. Consistent mealtimes will develop better and more consistent eating habits for the entire family.

How to Live with Your Children and Like Them

Chapter 15
Understanding Sex

Every human has a built-in drive, desire or urge for sex, and these feelings increase as the child matures into puberty. During the early years, children often have a curiosity about their own genitalia or those of the opposite sex.

Some parents misconstrue this curiosity as an abnormal sex drive which will get out of control as the child advances in age. The parents fail to realize that the child's thinking does not take in all the ramifications of sex which would go on in the adult's mind. The young child merely views the genitalia as a curious object he has just recently discovered. He does not think of these objects any differently than any other new gadget or toy.

Parents must free themselves from being too emotional in this area. They must help the child to understand the principle while treating the subject as casually as other new learning experiences, such as tying a shoe or managing a knife or fork. The child, in turn, will then not see sex as a big deal, and will move on from it to something else.

Parents often try too hard in this area and go into lengthy discussions about the "birds and bees" and many implications the child cannot understand. This whets his curiosity more than is necessary. Giving him too much information about sex earlier than his age and mind are able to comprehend does more damage than good, as it starts him off on the footpath earlier than his mental maturity can handle. A good rule of thumb is to hold off the teaching of sex until the child expresses a desire to be informed.

A parent must recognize that sex is not bad, is not sinful, under the proper conditions. Our physical and psychological makeup cries out for a relationship of this nature. With the proper companion in marriage, it can be beautiful. Sex in marriage should be an experience wherein either husband or wife can come and receive comforting reassurance, status, security, and, most of all, a deep and honest love.

Sex is self-destructive when it is given away permissively, out of wedlock, without the covenants of a marriage. One cannot find reassurance, status, security, and an in-depth love with a stranger in the night. As people practice sex permissively out of wedlock, they achieve merely physical gratification. Without the psychological well-being satisfied, their experience soon becomes an exercise in frustration.

Sex, then, should be a sacred and beautiful element which cements the marriage together and provides strength and well-being to cope with the stress and strain of the environment around us.

In teaching children, it is not possible to tell them truthfully that they cannot have sex feelings, drives, or desires, because everyone is born with these natural feelings. We can teach our children the importance of "how-to's," however, of governing these urges so that they will not be misused or abused. Children who are taught how to manage their emotions, actions and feelings in childhood, and to be in control, seem to have less problems of immorality as teenagers or adults. Those children who are constantly testing and fudging rules and getting away with improper behavior in childhood take these personality traits with them to adulthood and are prime targets for deviate sex behavior as adults. Children must learn certain principles while they are young.

Just giving a child information or helping him become knowledgeable about sex and its many ramifications will not get the job done. Parents have caused more damage than good by giving their children knowledge about sex when they are too emotionally immature to handle it. When this is the case, the child's knowledge only encourages the next step to experimentation.

Never in the history of man has venereal disease run so rampant or illegitimate pregnancies, abortions, marriage breakups, or suicide rates taken their toll so heavily upon society. Almost all of these tragedies came about because of the so-called "freedom of sex" which was supposed to bring about more pleasure and happiness for the human race. The truly happy person in life is the one who is in control of himself and the environment around him. He experiences an inner peace with himself, void of conflict, heartache, fear and guilt, those culprits which destroy the soul and corrupt the mind.

In the past ten years, the number of homosexuals I have seen in therapy has increased noticeably. In a great many cases, the pattern seems to follow a trend wherein the youth has the first experience of homosexuality in his early teens. A close association generally develops in which the individuals are exposed to each other at summer camp, slumber parties, or outings, in campus dormitories, or by swimming in the nude, or having sleeping quarters separate or away from the family. The sex play first takes place by the individuals fondling or caressing each other. Following this comes the act of masturbating with each other, and then finally come various sexual acts. After they have indulged in the interplay, both persons feel a deep-seated psychological effect. The excitement and thrills of the moment are soon replaced by anxiety, fear, and guilt. Although most will not admit it except in therapy, a homosexual person is an unhappy person. He sees himself as being different or abnormal and is often depressed and frightened.

Man is superior to the animal because he has a brain with which to think, reason and govern himself. People who allow themselves to let their emotions or appetites get out of control haven't learned how to govern themselves. It isn't that they lack the ability but that they need help in learning how to handle the problem emotionally.

A seventeen-year-old boy was referred for therapy by the police department. He was a well-mannered person with better than average intelligence. He was a good student in school, had a religious background, was a leader among his friends, and seemed to have everything going for him. He would not cheat, steal, tell lies, or in any way offend another person. He seemed a gentleman in every respect. In fact he managed himself very well in all areas of life except one. In this one area he functioned very poorly, and as a result he was about to be sentenced to a long term in jail. He mismanaged his sex drives to the degree that they were beginning to destroy him.

His problem would first start in the thinking process. He would let his mind ponder, dwell and fantasize on sex until he would build his emotions up so high that they would take over and direct his actions. He would disrobe himself after dark and prowl up and down peeking in bedroom windows. On one occasion he was shot at and narrowly missed being killed. One of the first statements he made in therapy was: "I can't help myself. I was born this way and can't help it." I asked the question, "If a person can take control of one set of appetites or drives such as stealing or temper tantrums, can't he control sex drives too?" The answer was obvious. When a person really decides to come to terms with the problem and wants to change, he can. This is best taught by a child's parents.

This young man is now functioning sufficiently well that he is being released from probation and is leading a normal life. When bad thoughts creep in he has learned to control them by reading a book, taking a bicycle ride, calling a friend, or doing something that will change the pattern of thought to a more constructive way of performing. He has learned that when an individual is in control of his thoughts and emotions this is a good world to be a part of.

Other cases I have known involve permissive girls who claim they are "oversexed." This claim really has nothing to do with the problem. Almost always the juvenile is lonely, troubled, looking for a relationship in which she can find some kind of acceptance with a companion. Usually her involvement in the family is under stress and strain. And it's so easy for a girl to gain acceptance in a relationship with a male if she is willing to indulge in sex play. She doesn't have to be good looking, have a good personality, be intelligent, or have a good figure; so she can drift into this kind of a relationship very easily without working hard to achieve it.

After she has achieved this type of relationship on the basis of sex only, however, the girl receives little or nothing back other than the physical gratification, and often even this is not present. To repeat, this relationship gives no status, security, reassurance or in-depth love on an ongoing basis, and the experience soon becomes an exercise in frustration. This enhances the loneliness even more as the girl passes from one companion to another.

Thus we see how vital it is for parents to teach their children, first, to control emotions and actions; and second, to understand sex. No one can substitute-teach sex. For example, school teachers do not accurately know the child's mental and emotional maturity, nor can they normally have the child's interest at heart as the parent does. If more careful teaching by parents took place during early child-rearing years, many later heartaches could easily be avoided for both parent and child.

How to Live with Your Children and Like Them

Chapter 16

Runaways

"This family makes me sick! You won't let me have any fun. I can't exercise my rights or my freedom, so I'm going to run away! I'm going to go where I can live by myself!"

This angry outburst has been heard often where troubled children have been reared. Another familiar outcry is: "You wait till I'm eighteen years old, and I'll leave this house and never return. You're always trying to control my life."

To hear their own children threaten to leave home causes panic in most parents. They immediately envision the dangers that lie waiting out in society for unsuspecting children who are vulnerable to the world's temptations. The thought of their unprotected child out on the streets usually results in the parents' compromising principles or standards at almost any cost to keep the goodwill of the child and have him remain at home.

Is it any wonder then that Joe soon learns to use this weapon to control his parents? Scores of therapy cases involving runaways verify this fact. The number one reason why children run away is to manipulate or control parents. This method of control has been especially popular since about 1970.

One of the major factors which contributes to the runaway situation and actually encourages such behavior are the many adults who see themselves as do-gooders. They open their doors to the troubled runaways, welcome them with open arms, and offer them living quarters until they can come to terms with their parents.

Nothing could encourage a runaway situation more. At the neighbor's, the runaway finds a warm home and a sympathetic audience. Always the runaway tells tales of how badly he was abused at home, while the do-gooder swallows the story and harbors him without checking out the facts. With this kind of supportive help, running away becomes easy. Almost always someone outside the family is handy and ready to take in the runaway. Most do-gooders have sincere intentions and feel a sense of satisfaction that they are helping mankind, when in fact they are putting fuel on the fire.

Some might argue, "But that's better than the child's being out on the streets!" And we answer, "Is it?" If no one befriended or cared for the runaway, perhaps his only alternative would be to go home and work out the problems with his mother and father.

A good example of this was Blair, who was being reared by a natural father and a stepmother. Blair's own mother was killed in a car accident when he was five years old and the stepmother came into the family when he was six. The stepmother was a warm, well-meaning, kind person who tried too hard to win Blair's approval and affections. Blair mistook kindness for weakness and abused the love she radiated to him.

At fifteen Blair was truant from school most of the time, failing in all his classes. He was using drugs and was rebellious and abusive to his parents and family members. He would not perform duties or chores at home and refused to be part of the family.

When his father firmly insisted that he stay in school, Blair ran away from home and lived with another family who had a troubled boy Blair's age. Blair told his story to the do-good mother: he was unloved at home, misunderstood, abused by having to attend church against his wishes, and required to do all the work in the family. The do-gooder bought the story and then called Blair's parents, berating them for nearly an hour. She appointed herself as the one to put Blair on his feet. She felt he just needed someone to understand and trust him.

The first two weeks Blair used his best manners and performed quite well in the new surroundings. Then the newness wore off, he stayed out prowling most of the night, slept till noon, demanded meals at all hours, took the family car without permission, and smuggled "pot" into the house. In all his escapades, Blair took the teen-age son with him.

At the end of a month, the haven of love for the runaway had turned into bedlam. Mrs. K. called Blair's folks again, this time pleading with them to take him home. When they didn't respond, she called the school principal to declare him truant and have him taken from the house. The school ignored her request because she had sheltered other truants before and had lied for them. Finally, in desperation, the family called the police, and Blair was placed in a detention home. Two weeks there had a sobering effect upon him. When Blair was released to come home and given back his freedom, he was ready to function as a worthwhile family member.

From the cases I have seen in therapy it appears that 85 percent of runaways go no farther than a mile or two from home. After they have established themselves as runaways, the usual pattern is to send notes home (with no return address) stating how bad they feel to have parents who don't care about them and won't give them freedom to do their own thing. They blame their parents for the runaway situation.

Along with notes, sometimes come phone calls, the runaway being careful not to identify where he is staying. Sometimes he sends a chum to the house to see if Mother and Father are paining enough to let the offspring back into the family on his own terms. Usually parents are so relieved and happy to have the runaway home that they will settle at any price, only to have the returned teenager abuse or control the family even more.

When parents can be helped so they do not respond to this kind of extortion and can see this runaway period as a time when the family is free from turmoil, anger, and struggle, strange things happen. The runaway learns that he has not been missed that much, and he sees that the family is not at home moping and crying for his return at any price. All the power and thunder of running away has been thwarted. It's no fun any longer when it's clearly not paying off.

Children really do not enjoy camping out or living with strangers. They are usually poorly cared for, have to live in the same clothing they left home in, and bunk with someone else or sleep on the floor. They usually have to take second best in the new situation.

It is unwise for parents to chase their children about in the community from one hideout to another. If parents will not get caught up in the urge to go and find them, but instead will wait it out and not respond to their desperate need to bring them home, they will work through the problem much quicker. It is important to let the child make the first move to come home, for when he arrives at the front door wanting to come back into the family, *that is the teaching moment for parents.*

At this moment the parents' response is tremendously important. The most meaningful dialogue might go like this: "Son, you want to be admitted back into the family, and we as parents want you back, so we both want the same thing. However, if you are given this privilege, how are you going to manage yourself in the future? What can we expect from you as a family member?"

At this point the parents should get some basic commitments from the runaway. If he fades back into the family under his own terms, parents have accomplished nothing toward changing his behavior. So, before letting him back into the home, the parent should go through the rules of the family with him and let *him* respond to each rule as to how he sees himself functioning. If a parent verbally tells him how he is to manage and he is not making any commitments on his own, he could say to himself, "Those are your ideas, Father, but I'm not going to be a part of them."

If he refuses to make commitments and is still angry or rebellious, this tells the parent that he has not really taken control of his emotions or actions and is not ready to come home to be a worthwhile family member. In this case, admittance to the home and family should be denied, because he is only coming home to antagonize people and to disrupt the harmony of the household. If there has been a genuine recovery from hostility, however, and there is but a speck of willingness to try to make amends for wrongdoing, it would be sad not to let him come back and try. Any child who is genuinely willing to try should be given every opportunity to do so with all the help and encouragement parents can muster.

A harmful trap some parents fall into is that of bluffing the child when the subject of running away comes up. The child starts out by bluffing the parent with the statement, "I'm going to run away." The parents retaliate by saying, "I'll help you pack your bag."

Neither party wants this to happen but each feels he must outbluff the other in order to save face. So the child takes the situation a little further by getting the bag for the parents to pack. Each hopes the other will relent, but neither does. The bag is packed and the child is on his way out of the door. Mother bluffs a little more by saying, "I'll walk you to the bus so you can go." Both feel caught up in the game and can't turn back. They walk to the bus, still pushing each other, and here the situation becomes frightening.

Suddenly the bus appears. The door opens and the child disappears inside. The bus rolls out of sight, leaving Mother desperate and the offspring sick at what is happening.

A much better way to handle the situation when Joe says he is going to run away would be to express these feelings: "I can understand that you are very angry at this moment, and I know you are experiencing very real feelings that you want to leave. However, even though you feel this way, I don't think you need to act this way, and I'm going to expect that you stop it!"

Now there is no bluffing or power struggle for either to get caught up in. Joe knows exactly where Father stands on the issue of running away. He is expected not to do so, and that settles the issue. Helping the child run away belies the true feelings of child and parent. Neither wants a runaway situation, but both get caught up in the emotion and suddenly, to the sorrow of each, it has happened.

So we see that dealing with the runaway problem is no different from dealing with any other kind of misbehavior. The parent is the authority in charge, so it is up to him to take control and firmly reinforce the standards expected from and the limitations imposed upon the family members.

Chapter 17

The Sexually Abused Child

A parent reported to a family therapist that her six-year-old daughter, Katie, came home from spending the night at a friend's house and was upset and seemed to cry for no reason at all. The mother attributed the behavior to her daughter being tired, so early in the afternoon she put her to bed for a nap. After the daughter woke up, the mother said she was quiet and moody. The pattern of being withdrawn, moody, or angry continued for several weeks, causing the mother to seek professional help. She thought she was doing something to cause the daughter to act out of sorts. The mother eventually reported to the therapist that Katie had been molested by an older brother of her friend with whom Katie had spent the night. Another girl had told her parents of being abused by the same boy, and word got back to Katie's mother. She then asked Katie if she had been molested also. Katie broke into tears and said she had; and then asked when she was going to be punished. The mother reassured Katie that she was not in trouble. Katie began to heal.

147

One of the most devastating things that can occur in a child's life is to be abused sexually. Sexual abuse can be defined as a person touching or fondling a child in the genital area or in a sexual manner. Unfortunately, it is an all too often occurrence today. The act is typically carried out by a person significantly older than the child and is usually a family member, or a close friend of the family.

Some of the questions asked by parents regarding sexual abuse are, "How can I tell if my child has been abused?" "How can I prevent it?" "What happens to a child after being abused?" and, "How can I help my child after such a terrible thing has happened to her?" Although this is an unpleasant subject to discuss, it must be addressed because of its frequency. If handled in a healthy way, a sexual abuse encounter can either be avoided, or worked through so the victim can live an unencumbered life. Each of these questions will be addressed in this chapter with the goal of restoring a sense of safety and self-worth to the victim.

First of all, let us explore how we can determine that a child has been sexually abused. All behavior has meaning in understanding people. The trick is to understand what it means, especially if the person is not willing to reveal the meaning. The most common behaviors reported by parents of children who have been sexually abused are severe mood changes or swings and withdrawal from family and friends, and frequent displays of temper and anger.

Second, how can we prevent abuse from happening? It is not necessary for parents to spend time explaining in great detail what sexual abuse is. Parents who do so are likely to confuse the child with terms not easily understood. Also, vivid and detailed descriptions can leave a child frightened and unsure around people.

The best approach is to tell the child, in language she can understand is that no one is to touch her in the genital area (privates). Also, children who have been molested will usually report being told by the perpetrator that if she tells anyone, she will be in real trouble, or that no one will believe her. Another ploy used by the perpetrator to avoid being caught is to tell the child that if she tells, he will hurt her or the family. A rational thinking adult knows that these things will never happen, because the molester is a cowardly person. But children do not understand this. All they know is that the person is big, has some type of power, and that adults usually mean what they say. The scare tactic is hard for a child to ignore.

When talking to children with the idea of avoiding sexual abuse, reassure them that not only are they not to let anyone touch them where they shouldn't, but that whatever the person says is a lie. Reassure children that they will always be protected, and that if it really happened, they will be believed. When children truly understand this they will not be reluctant to tell an adult that someone is trying to molest them, or that they have been molested.

Third, what do we know about what happens to children after they are molested? Usually, the child first feels frightened about somehow being in trouble for what has happened. This is what happened to Katie when she was molested by her friend's older brother. She knew that what happened was somehow wrong, but she was not mature enough to reason that she would not be in trouble, but that the older boy was the person in the wrong. Because of the guilt feelings, the child becomes frightened and will typically act out the guilt through anger and defensiveness, or by withdrawing from people. These feelings put the person in the role of a victim.

One adult patient initially came in for help with depression and anxiety. She eventually admitted that she had been molested when ten years old, and that she was so consumed by what happened that she could not concentrate on anything. She repeatedly had nightmares about people trying to hurt her. As a result, she said that she had such a fear of being hurt by people that she became a person who was easily taken advantage of by others. Most molestation victims report spending a great amount of time dwelling on what happened, which leads to depression and anxiety. Because thinking about the problem keeps it foremost in the person's mind, the resulting emotions and feelings can become real to the individual.

Finally, how do we help children who have been molested? The first step in helping the child heal is for the parent to come to terms with his own feelings so those feelings do not interfere with helping his child. Feeling guilty is one problem. Most often parents report feeling guilty for not being there to protect their children. While in therapy, one father said that he felt so badly about his son's molestation that he wished it had happened to him rather than his son. Feeling sorry is another problem. Parents tend to feel sorry for the child. As was explained in the first of the book, if parents allow their feelings to take over, the ability to teach is severely compromised.

Parents must realize that the deed cannot be erased. We cannot pretend that it never happened, nor can the child. In order for the child to heal, we must focus on the resulting behaviors that interfere with the child functioning positively in the people world. As was mentioned, when a molested child becomes frightened, she will manifest unhealthy behaviors in order to protect herself from further harm. If parents allow these unhealthy behaviors to continue, the child's mental and emotional state will worsen. Parents must help the child by teaching her to function in an acceptable way despite her feelings. This is necessary for several reasons. She needs to learn that she has control of her life. She must learn that not all people are bad. She must prove to herself that she is a worthwhile person, not bad or dirty.

It helps parents to understand that the child is not guilty of anything, and that their child literally had no control over the situation. Most children say that when they were approached by the abuser and while being abused they thought that if they said "no," they would be hurt or in trouble. Children look at people older than themselves as authorities, or as with such strength, that they have no say in what happens to them. When children are assured by loving parents that they are not at fault and will not be trouble, they usually begin to heal emotionally. Once the child is helped with this part of her thinking, she will be in a position to be taught to manage her emotions and behaviors.

To be an effective teacher, the parent must not allow his feelings to interfere with the teaching process. Most parents say that they feel sorry for the child and thus make excuses for her or make special allowances for poor behavior. One young lady told her story of abuse and said that she was allowed to do just about anything she wanted whenever she asked. If she were initially told "no," she would pout and act sad until her parents felt guilty and gave in to her requests. She eventually realized that she was acting differently than her friends and was being treated in a way that made her feel less adequate than her friends.

The parents must teach the child to act in a healthy manner in spite of what she has gone through. This is done by letting the child know how she is expected to act and then invite her to practice it, until it becomes natural. An example is teaching her to overcome her timid feelings, which are very common among abuse victims. Father and Mother must tell her that she needs to interact with people. She must start talking to her friends. In the beginning, she will likely protest and try to get out of it by playing on their sympathies. When the parents are able to put aside their sorry feelings, they can insist that she start interacting with her friends, and hold her accountable to their request. As the child eventually starts interacting, parents can review the experience and give helpful encouragement and advice. The parents can then look for other opportunities for their child to do things with peers, and again help her work through her fears by once more insisting that she do things with them. They must go through this teaching process again, and again until the child is able to initiate healthy interactions with others on her own.

This same concept applies to interacting with adults. Lori, an abuse victim, was terrified to be around adult men. It was interfering with her schooling, because her teacher was a man. She was originally thought to have a school phobia, but it was later found that she thought her teacher would hurt her because in her mind all grown men were molesters. Initially, without their knowing why she acted as she did, her parents learned how to firmly, but lovingly insist that she go to school. They also held her accountable to talk with her teacher as well as other adult men. Once she overcame the fear of men, the conflict she was feeling dissipated and she was able to explain to her parents why she was fearful of men.

While the author was working in an adolescent psychiatric unit, he quickly observed that the majority of female patients had a history of some type of sexual abuse. They all revealed that they felt like victims and were powerless over their fates. Most of the girls had not told anyone about their plight. The therapist helped them see that as long as they did not report the abuse to the authorities, they were victims. When they made a report, they soon gained a feeling of empowerment and control over their lives. Some of these girls had to face their assailants in court, a frightening experience. Once the ordeal was over, they all said they felt they had no need to fear the person or others like them ever again. If they had not reported the incident, they would have remained feeling helpless and would have acted like victims.

The most important thing to understand when helping a child who has been sexually abused is that the resulting thoughts, feelings, and emotions are extremely damaging, but can be managed. If the child is not taught to manage these feelings, her life will be miserable and she and those around her will suffer.

The most important thing to remember is that the past cannot be relived. A child can still learn how to function in a normal and healthy way without fear. As Mother and Father reassure her that she is not in trouble, that she is safe, and that she can trust most people, she will begin to build a bright future. Most importantly, parents must understand that they cannot allow their child to act on the negative feelings resulting from the abuse, but they can learn to act as other healthy children, in spite of the past.

Chapter 18

Parents' Relationship in Rearing Children

One of the major stress factors in a marriage relationship is the conflict which often comes between husband and wife in regard to rearing children. Many arguments occur, especially concerning approaches to discipline.

Ill will toward a mate about the discipline used with their children will often cause the other mate to do the opposite to make up to the children for the wrong he or she feels was inflicted by the spouse. For instance, if Father feels Mother is unfair and is too harsh in her disciplining of the children, he will try to compensate by being extra loose and lax. It reacts on the children like an off-balance set of scales. One is too tight because he feels he must make up for the other's laxness. The one that is lax feels she must perform in this way because of the tight rein the other mate uses. It is a vicious circle in which the ability for the parents to teach the children is nil.

When parents get into this kind of power struggle with each other, the children use such situations to manipulate or pit one against the other. This can destroy the family and the marriage.

Without fully realizing it, many parents choose up sides as to who will be the disciplinarian and who will be the "good guy." The supposed "good guy" sets out to be the buddy or the chum, thinking all the while that this is the way to win the children's love.

This will not do. Both parents need to be teachers, each being willing to help the child whenever the help is needed. Too often we hear of Mother putting up with misbehavior through the day while she threatens the child with Father when he arrives home from work. When this situation occurs, the child sees Mother as a weak person who cannot cope or function on her own but must have the supportive help of another adult. This causes the child to lose admiration or respect for Mother. The child minds when Father is present; but the moment he leaves, Mother's word is ineffective and meaningless. The offspring pays no attention to her.

This is a bad situation for Father because he is made to deal with problems which developed through the day and have grown cold by the time he arrives on the scene. He has no first-hand knowledge as to what has happened and is often caught up in putting his wife on the level of the child, having to hear both sides of the story and then make a decision in the favor of one or the other. Certainly Mother's feeling incapable of coping and having to wait for Father does not create a good image of her as a parent for the child.

While I was conducting group therapy with twenty-six parents, it was very clear that one couple had selected a role for each of them to play with the children. Mother was the good person and was very permissive with their four children—allowing, condoning, and putting up with poor behavior. Father found himself having to be the one to take control of the children, and he sometimes had to over-discipline to compensate for the mother's laxness. This would exasperate Father, so he would try many gimmicks to goad Mother into taking responsibility, such as leaving the room and pretending not to hear what was going on. On each occasion, however, he would get very anxious about his wife's ineffectiveness and would end up by interceding with disgust.

Near the halfway point in group therapy, the father, who was in the Naval Reserve, received orders to return to sea duty. Mother and the children would be by themselves for more than nine months. Suddenly a drastic change came over Mother. This once-permissive parent, who was very weak and lax about disciplining, completely reversed herself and became even more forceful than Father was. This was a shock to the children, and they were confused at the sudden change in behavior.

I noticed the change and wondered what was happening to Mother. Her answer was simple—Father was no longer present to pick up the slack. He was no longer there to set the limits so she could take the easy way out. Her only recourse now was to do the disciplining herself.

Another damaging factor in the family relationship results when mother chooses one or two children to be her favorites and they can do no wrong. Father chooses a favorite or two also, and the game begins. One parent gives support to his favorites to undermine the others. The children are pawns in the hands of immature parents who destroy the family's happiness. The cause of this situation usually stems back to the parents' inability to get along with each other. They use the children as an additional lever in manipulating each other. As the unknowing children lend their weight to one parent or another, resentment and even hate surface between the parents.

Divorced parents are often very foolish in the way they relate to the children who are caught in the middle of the problem. The mother and father remarry and try to establish a new life for themselves. The children, then, are usually shuttled back and forth from one parent to the other, each wanting "equal time." Both parents feel sorry for the children and want to win their favor.

The results? The offspring are pampered, over-indulged, and spoiled until their personalities are incorrigible. The children are not taught responsibility, how to get along with people, or how to handle emotions or actions. They usually grow up to be complete failures. Ironically enough, of all times the children need help in learning how to manage themselves is in a divorced situation. It ends up that they get less teaching in this situation than at any other time.

Adopted children also may present emotional problems for families, especially for parents. Counselors' files are full of problem children who are adopted. One of the primary reasons is that the parents of adopted children try too hard in their role of parenting. Our natural children are our own flesh and blood, very much a part of us both physically and emotionally. We are therefore prone to accept them into the family without undue psychological stress or strain. This is not true with the adopted child, who arrives more as an outsider wanting to get in.

The parents also want the adopted child in the inner family circle, and they try too hard. The parents often walk on eggs with these children, feeling that they have to keep proving their love and acceptance to the child. When parents feel anxious or unsure with the adopted child, the child senses this and uses it against the parents, to manipulate and control. This in turn causes conflict and turmoil, not only among the other children but between the parents.

To avoid marital conflict over rearing children, both parents need to recognize the following facts, which in effect summarize some of the basic principles discussed already:

Children are basically durable, sturdy and strong. They are not so fragile that they tend to break or shatter at the slightest provocation.

Children need to be given responsibilities early in life to assure growth and development. It is impossible for them to learn unless they have the opportunities to try. In arranging this, parents should not bask in the sun while the children do all the work. On the contrary, the major objective should be to teach responsibility through precept and example. Children must be taught how to take directions and how to accept a task and complete it.

The parent who denies the child the basic experience of first functioning well in the family is interfering with his maturation into adulthood.

To take over and constantly do for the child denies him the essential lessons of life. In the adult world he will not be treated this way but will be required to perform.

To reiterate, parents who want to shelter, over-protect, and *do* for the offspring are certainly not doing their child a favor, as later years will prove.

One might think that to win the love of a child would necessitate putting up with misbehavior. The child, however, does not see this kind of permissiveness as love. Rather, he sees it as weakness and will use it against the adult.

When misbehavior is tolerated, trouble brews between child and parent and, most of all, between the father and the mother. And when the relationship of the husband and wife deteriorates, it is impossible to properly rear the children.